JAMIE SNYDER

THOU SHALL NOT

FREEDOM TO STRIP AWAY
THE "NOTS"
AND DISCOVER WHAT
GOD REALLY WANTS

David C Cook®
transforming lives together

THOU SHALL
Published by David C Cook
4050 Lee Vance View
Colorado Springs, CO 80918 U.S.A.

David C Cook Distribution Canada
55 Woodslee Avenue, Paris, Ontario, Canada N3L 3E5

David C Cook U.K., Kingsway Communications
Eastbourne, East Sussex BN23 6NT, England

The graphic circle C logo is a registered trademark of David C Cook.

LCCN 2014943143
ISBN 978-1-4347-0766-6
eISBN 978-0-7814-1240-7

© 2014 Jamie Snyder
Published in association with the literary agency:
The Gates Group, www.the-gates-group.com

The Team: Alex Field, Caitlyn Carlson, Carly Razo, Nick Lee, Karen Athen
Cover Design: Amy Konyndyk
Cover Photo: iStockphoto

Printed in the United States of America
First Edition 2014

1 2 3 4 5 6 7 8 9 10

063014

For my Hazel girl,
I pray you change the rest of the world
the way you have changed mine.

CONTENTS

ACKOWLEDGMENTS

My name may be on the front cover, but there are many others whose could be as well. Names of people who believed in, invested in, prayed for, corrected, and polished the *Thou Shall* message. Names such as Alex, Ingrid, John, Caitlyn, Carly, Don, and multiple others.

To all of you I share these sincere, yet insufficient words: thank you. Without you the *Thou Shall* message would have never moved from theory into reality. My prayer for each of you is that you know a Thou Shall God is pursuing you and wants to be pursued by you. A God who is not impressed by mere passivity, but a God who passionately, desperately wants to carry out His will here on earth as it is in heaven, and wants His followers to do the same.

Part I

STRIPPING AWAY
THE NOTS

Chapter 1

FAVORITE WORDS

What are your favorite words?

Favorite words are the ones always ready to roll off the tip of your tongue. The ones you are known for saying the most often. The words you resort to using when you are unsure what else to say.

Most of us would likely have a difficult time determining what our favorite words are. A quick way to find out? Ask the people who know you best. Go ahead—see what they say. You may love their responses; you may loathe their responses. Either way, you just might discover your favorite words.

Favorite words matter. They do not simply shape our language; they reveal the shape of our heart. And they do not just reflect the pattern of our speech; they reflect the pattern of our mind. Favorite words, whatever they may be, say so much about who we are and what we are all about.

Have you ever wondered about God's favorite words? I'm pretty sure most people haven't. But several months ago, I did.

Now, I didn't sit down with the intention of determining God's favorite words, but as I evaluated the landscape of modern Christianity, I concluded that most of us have a common misconception on this subject. If asked, many people would probably say God's favorite words are "I love you." That is a nice Sunday-school answer, and perhaps at some level theologically appropriate. Yet when you look at the lives of many Christians—including mine for many years—"I love you" doesn't seem to be what we believe is on the tip of God's tongue.

I was raised in an über-conservative nondenominational Christian church in central Kansas. There was nothing unusual about the church. The building had a steeple, stained-glassed windows, and red carpet on the floors in the auditorium (red carpet must be biblical—I think the verse is tucked away somewhere in 2 Titus). My church was filled with very simple people—primarily middle-class families who lived comfortable lives. From my earliest memories I attended church on Sunday mornings, Sunday evenings, and Wednesday nights. As a child I did not believe in the Easter Bunny, Santa Claus, or the Tooth Fairy (though I did believe pro wrestling was real), but I always believed in God.

In my early years, almost everything I knew about God I learned from a flannel board. Do you remember flannel boards? If not, you didn't miss much, but for the sake of the story, I'll fill you in: A flannel board is a piece of flannel—usually baby blue—that has been stretched over the surface of a board. Bible characters cut out of felt stick to the baby-blue flannel, forming a captivating picture or scene that illustrates the biblical story being taught. Flannel board was kind of like the HDTV of the 1980s. Kind of.

I remember learning from a flannel board about God creating the universe in six days; Adam and Eve and the garden of Eden (only years later did I realize why flannel-board Adam and Eve were always hiding behind a bush with huge grins on their faces); God splitting the Red Sea to allow Moses and the Israelites to cross on dry land; and the Ten Commandments. I cannot remember exactly how the teacher depicted the scene—I am sure it was cute—but I learned how Moses went up on the mountaintop to meet with God. And how on that mountaintop, God shared with Moses what we affectionately— or not so affectionately, depending on who you are—have referred to as the Ten Commandments.[1]

I. Thou shalt have no other gods before me.

II. Thou shalt not make unto thee a graven image, nor any likeness of any thing that is in heaven above, or that is in the earth beneath, or that is in the water under the earth.

III. Thou shalt not take the name of Jehovah thy God in vain.

IV. Remember the sabbath day, to keep it holy.

V. Honor thy father and thy mother.

VI. Thou shalt not kill.

VII. Thou shalt not commit adultery.

VIII. Thou shalt not steal.

IX. Thou shalt not bear false witness against thy neighbor.

X. Thou shalt not covet thy neighbor's house.

Now, if we created a list of images or ideas people associate with Christianity, the cross would probably be at the top, but I think the stone tablets containing the Ten Commandments would be next. In fact, people who know almost nothing about the Bible are usually still able to recognize the Ten Commandments, especially these three words: *Thou Shall Not.*

This is where a real problem begins in the Christian faith.

Don't get me wrong—I am glad people both within and outside the church are familiar with the Ten Commandments, if for no other reason than because these commandments are the very words of God. However, my concern is that too many people subconsciously believe God's favorite words are "Thou Shall Not."

Here's an important question to consider: If someone believes God's favorite words are "Thou Shall Not," how would that belief impact the way he or she approaches a life of faith?

Theoretically speaking, if a person believed God's favorite words were "Thou Shall Not," then that person would primarily view God as the Great Referee in the Sky—the One who is always lurking, just waiting to blow His whistle at the slightest rule infraction. If a Christian believed that is who God is and that is what God does, then naturally life and faith would be a matter of trying to avoid the whistle. In other words, a person would quickly learn to exert most of his or her energy on avoiding rule infractions. To use theological language, if someone viewed God in this way, his or her highest priority in life and faith would be sin avoidance (theoretically speaking, of course).

I do not think there is anything theoretical about this perspective of God and faith, though. In fact, on some level, many if not most Christians seem to view Him this way. While I do not think it is a conscious decision, the evidence suggests that this flawed view is prevalent. **If and when someone views the purpose of the Christian life as a matter of avoiding sin, something has gone terribly wrong.**

In approaching this issue, I know I am treading on dangerous ground. One could easily assume that I am at the very least minimizing sin and at the most treating sin flippantly. In no way am I trying to communicate that sin of any size or shape is not serious. Quite the opposite—sin is dead serious. The collective sin of every man, woman, and child who has ever lived sent Jesus to die in the most painful, humiliating fashion this world has ever known. Sin could not be more serious and could not matter more to God.

However, the nature of the Christian life is not about sin avoidance. Living life this way cheapens the call we have received to follow Jesus and communicates a lack of understanding of who God is and what God is like. God does not wear a striped shirt and a whistle, and He doesn't delight in catching us in the middle of a rule infraction.

THE GOD OF NOTS

If someone were reading through the Bible for the first time and began in the Old Testament, he or she might mistakenly develop the impression that God enjoys hunting down rule breakers. In fact, he or she would need to read only the first few chapters of Genesis to form this impression of God.

When you read the story of Noah in Genesis 6 and watch God unleashing worldwide destruction in response to the sin of mankind,

He does seem to be a bit of a tyrant. Genesis 6 may be the first time we see God enact corporal punishment in response to sin, but it's certainly not the last time. Throughout the Old Testament, we often find God with blood on His hands as the result of killing people. Sometimes it's large groups of people; other times it is individuals. Sometimes the people committed sins we would tend to categorize as major sins; other times the sins committed seemed harmless.

In Numbers 15, God definitely seems to be eager to throw a flag and blow the whistle. He had just handed down the commandments to the Israelites, and you don't have to read beyond this narrative to see just how serious He was about these rules.

> While the Israelites were in the wilderness, a man was found gathering wood on the Sabbath day. Those who found him gathering wood brought him to Moses and Aaron and the whole assembly, and they kept him in custody, because it was not clear what should be done to him. Then the LORD said to Moses, "The man must die. The whole assembly must stone him outside the camp." So the assembly took him outside the camp and stoned him to death, as the LORD commanded Moses. (Num. 15:32–36)

So the man gathers a bit of wood on a Sabbath afternoon, and in the next moment, he is stoned by his friends and family. God did not intervene; God ordered the stoning. If gathering wood on Sunday afternoon gets you stoned, then I'd better duck and cover because

I have done far worse on Sunday afternoons—not to mention the things I have done Monday through Saturday.

I know I don't seem to be helping my case about the nature and character of God. In fact, stories like this one about the wood gatherer and others found all throughout the Old Testament seem to say that God is indeed a Thou Shall Not God.

But might God be widely misunderstood? I think so.

THE GOD OF GUARDRAILS

As I drive the highways of this nation, I always find two things along the way: guardrails and roadkill. I live in Kentucky, where some of my fellow residents view roadkill not as a nuisance but as a free meal. Seriously. Last fall as I was driving down an interstate, I saw an elderly man and woman standing behind their Cadillac. I began to slow down, thinking they were having car problems, but as I came closer, I realized they had just stopped to pick up dinner. They were tying a very large deer to the top of their trunk. That was my welcome-to-Kentucky moment. Poor Bambi.

Along almost every highway I have driven in America, I see free meals and guardrails. Sometimes the rails are shiny and new; other times they're rusty and fading. If you didn't know any better, guardrails would seem so restrictive. Their presence forces you to keep driving in a certain direction on a certain path; they contain you to a certain space. But in actuality, guardrails are present so you may live and live well. With guardrails in place, the risk of crossing into head-on traffic is significantly reduced—you would bump up against the guardrail before you could move into the path of danger. Bumping into the guardrail might leave a few scratches and dings on your car or truck, but the guardrail would likely save your life.

The Ten Commandments and other commandments of God are guardrails on the highway of life. If you do not fully understand their intention, the rules and commands of God could seem restrictive. Yet in reality God has given us commands and standards so we may live life to the fullest. The journey of life is not about the boundaries that have been set in place. The boundaries exist so we can safely complete the journey of faith. Believing that God is primarily a Thou Shall Not God is like thinking He is all about the guardrails. The reality is the only reason the Thou Shall Nots exist is because our sin nature would lead us off the pavement if the rails were not there. God has placed parameters in our lives so we can live. *Really* live.

Many Christians seem to believe that staying on the straight and narrow, following the rules, or staying away from the guardrails is the goal of the Christian life. Perhaps the reason this false concept is rarely addressed is because the idea has some credence. What could possibly be wrong about living life purposely avoiding sin?

When God placed Adam and Eve in the garden of Eden, He certainly did warn them to avoid the Tree of the Knowledge of Good and Evil, but that was not their primary purpose. They were told to tend to the land, be fruitful, and multiply. They were primarily assigned to be stewards of God's creation. Adam and Eve were not just to sustain the life that had already been established, but also to cultivate and multiply life. Indeed, God had warned them about the Tree of Knowledge of Good and Evil, but that warning was not intended to shape their lifestyle. It was to protect the lifestyle of freedom God had given them.

Unfortunately, when Adam and Eve chose to eat the forbidden fruit after being tempted by Satan, they did so because they had been convinced that their eyes would be opened and they would have the very mind of God. They believed they were one bite away from improving God's plan for mankind.

That's what sin is: an attempt to improve upon God's plan. The only problem, of course, is that God's ways are greater than our ways. "The foolishness of God is wiser than [our] wisdom" (1 Cor. 1:25). Sin promises to improve upon God's plan, but in reality sin always shatters the perfect plans of God. The first sin did just that. Adam and Eve, believing they could give God's plan an upgrade, indulged in the forbidden fruit, and immediately suffering and death sneaked through the back door of creation.

At the risk of oversimplifying the message of the Bible, after sin was initially chosen, God had to put many more restrictions in place to protect His people. If Adam and Eve had never chosen sin, the Old Testament law, including the Ten Commandments, would not have been necessary because people would have continued to naturally reflect the character of God, which can be summarized by the word *holy*.

Holiness.

The very purpose of creation was to bring glory to God, and in the absence of holiness, God does not receive any glory. Therefore, God values, longs for, demands, and expects holiness from His people. According to God's blueprints for the universe, holiness was to be woven into the fabric and flesh of creation. However, when sin was chosen in the garden of Eden, the clear reflection of God in His creation was shattered into a million pieces. Suddenly, where peace, harmony, and joy had ruled, pride, strife, and hate took the throne. Holiness had been the natural instinct of humanity, but that all changed after the first taste of forbidden fruit. However, humanity's failure in the garden did not in any way diminish God's passion for holiness. God still values, longs for, demands, and expects holiness from His people, and so understanding what it is and what it means to be holy is crucial to fulfilling His purpose for our lives.

For many years I would have explained holiness in terms of a Thou Shall Not list. I think this is the same perspective many Christians—at least subconsciously—have toward holiness.

In my first book, *Real*, I recounted the time I visited an abortion doctor in the town where I was living at the time—I'll call him Dr. A. I visited him simply for the purpose of apologizing to him for the way Christians had treated him throughout the years. He had been exposed to taunting, violence, and threats—none of which falls in line with following Jesus. I imagined I would stop by his office and, after requesting to meet with him, would be told he did not have time. But after speaking with the receptionist, I was escorted back to Dr. A's office. After explaining that I had no other agenda besides apologizing to him for the behavior of Christians, we settled into a very amicable conversation. At one point during the conversation, I said, "No doubt you have learned over the years what Christians are against, but do you know what we are *for?*" Dr. A sat in silence and then shook his head.

I was not surprised by his answer, but I was disappointed. Generally speaking, we as Christians have spent so much time, energy, and oxygen shouting about what we are against that many people have no idea what we stand for. This reality is disappointing, but I believe this truth is simply a symptom of another issue: we believe holiness is about not doing certain things. Probably subconsciously, somewhere along the way many of us have become convinced that God's favorite words are "Thou Shall Not."

So we are back to where we began—God is misunderstood.

Viewing God as a Thou Shall Not God causes us to miss out on who He is, what He is all about, and what we are to be all about. When you take a fresh and honest look at the God and faith of the Bible, the phrase "Thou Shall" would be a far more accurate description than "Thou Shall Not." One word changes everything.

This difference between the two perspectives of God and faith is no small thing, and changing viewpoints requires a massive paradigm shift. One perspective requires a person to manage a list of behaviors; the other requires a person to learn about the heart of God. One perspective demands a very cautious lifestyle; the other demands a messy life full of reckless love and scandalous grace. One perspective teaches that the end goal of faith is to get to the finish line with as few stains on our church clothes as possible; the other perspective demands that we get our church clothes wrinkled and our shoes scuffed. One perspective insults God; the other brings glory to Him.

REFLECT & DISCUSS

1. As you reflect on your faith journey, have you simply been trying to "avoid the whistle"?
2. If so, what factors contributed to your perspective of God as the Great Referee in the Sky? Family?

Spiritual leaders? Personal interpretation of Scripture?

3. Spend some time reflecting on building a faith where sin is taken seriously but sin avoidance is not the end goal.

4. Honestly evaluate your understanding of what it means to be holy. Do you define holiness primarily in terms of doing? Not doing? Both?

5. The Ten Commandments of God are not intended to oppress but to set free. However, they are not always viewed in this light. As you consider the commandments of God, do they seem to be oppressive or freeing?

PRAYER

Father, so many times and in so many ways I misunderstand who You are and what You are about. One of those ways is thinking about You as a Thou Shall Not God. Viewing You like this almost ensures that my faith will be built on the wrong foundation: sin avoidance instead of relationship. Though I am not capable of fully understanding Your nature and character, give me a sense of clarity so I may see You for who You really are. As I know You more completely, help me make appropriate adjustments in my life and faith to align with Your desires. Thank You for the grace You pour into my life in the midst of my misunderstandings. In Jesus's name.

Chapter 2

GOD ON THE MOVE

There is an undeniable relationship between our understanding of God and our expression of faith. We will work to emulate and apply to our lives whatever we believe God values most. If we thought God desired for us to juggle fire more than anything else, we would probably at least attempt to juggle fire. If we believed God desired for us to tame lions, we would seek to become skilled lion tamers. And if we believed God desired for us to walk on tightropes, we would sign up for tightrope-walking classes. Thankfully, God does not call us to any of these behaviors, and so none of them are necessary unless you are employed by a traveling circus. (If that's you, be careful.) Many Christians place the greatest emphasis on sin avoidance because they believe God places the highest value on sin avoidance.

Numerous times in the Old Testament, God used His prophets to chastise His chosen people, the Israelites. Certainly at times they were reprimanded for things they were doing that shouldn't be done. Specifically, God had to discipline His people over and over again for the sin of idolatry. From building golden calves to bowing to little-g gods to making sacrifices to idols, the Israelites were constantly dabbling in idolatry, and God never looked the other way. Worshipping anyone or anything other than the one true God is the essence of sin and rebellion, and so God consistently unleashed His fury as a result of their idolatrous ways. In the mind of God, idolatry was no doubt on the Thou Shall Not list. In fact, the first of the Ten Commandments addressed this very issue of idolatry. And when the people were finally allowed to enter into the Promised Land after forty years of wandering in the desert, they were warned numerous times and in numerous ways to avoid idolatry. Unfortunately, they didn't heed God's guidance. Clearly, idolatry and other behaviors were categorized as Thou Shall Nots. However, though God was adamant that His people should turn away from idolatry and other sinful ways, doing so was still not the primary purpose and mission of their lives as God's chosen people.

The same is true of the church. There are very specific behaviors God has commanded us to turn away from—sexual immorality, lying, gossip, slander, murder, and lust, just to name a few. If we wanted to, we could turn these commands into quite a long list of Thou Shall Nots. However, as I described earlier, these commands are guardrails; they are not intended to oppress us but rather to allow us to experience freedom and life.

Let's go back to the Old Testament. Though many times the Israelites were reprimanded for doing things they were not supposed to do, they were reprimanded just as often for things they should have done but didn't.

Hear the word of the LORD, you rulers of Sodom; listen to the instruction of our God, you people of Gomorrah! "The multitude of your sacrifices— what are they to me?" says the LORD. "I have more than enough of burnt offerings, of rams and the fat of fattened animals; I have no pleasure in the blood of bulls and lambs and goats. When you come to appear before me, who has asked this of you, this trampling of my courts? Stop bringing meaningless offerings! Your incense is detestable to me. New Moons, Sabbaths and convocations—I cannot bear your worthless assemblies. Your New Moon feasts and your appointed festivals I hate with all my being. They have become a burden to me; I am weary of bearing them. When you spread out your hands in prayer, I hide my eyes from you; even when you offer many prayers, I am not listening. Your hands are full of blood! Wash and make yourselves clean. Take your evil deeds out of my sight; stop doing wrong. Learn to do right; seek justice. Defend the oppressed. Take up the cause of the fatherless; plead the case of the widow. (Isa. 1:10–17)

Interestingly, the Israelites were making the prescribed sacrifices, they were observing the traditional meals and festivals, and they were in many ways adhering to the letter of the law. Knowing this, you would perhaps expect God to stand up from His throne and applaud the lifestyle of His people or put a gold star next to their names because they were in the temple at the appropriate times, participating in many seemingly righteous activities.

But applaud the Israelites God does not. This passage is a scathing message from God through His prophet Isaiah. Isaiah quotes God—whom the Bible later calls the personification of love—as saying that when His people pray to Him, He will hide His eyes and cover His ears. God is throwing a downright cosmic-sized fit.

Why is God so angry? If you read the last lines of the passage from Isaiah again, God is angry because of things the people are not doing. He commands them to "seek justice. Defend the oppressed. Take up the cause of the fatherless; plead the case of the widow." Reading between the lines, I gather that the Israelites were not seeking justice or encouraging the oppressed. They were not defending the cause of the fatherless or pleading the case of the widow.

This example of God ripping into His people for not caring about the same things He cares about was not an isolated incident. Actually, God was like a broken record about this:

> "Shout it aloud, do not hold back. Raise your voice
> like a trumpet. Declare to my people their rebellion
> and to the descendants of Jacob their sins. For day
> after day they seek me out; they seem eager to know
> my ways, as if they were a nation that does what is
> right and has not forsaken the commands of its God.
> They ask me for just decisions and seem eager for
> God to come near them. 'Why have we fasted," they
> say, 'and you have not seen it? Why have we humbled
> ourselves, and you have not noticed?' Yet on the day

of your fasting, you do as you please and exploit all your workers. Your fasting ends in quarreling and strife, and in striking each other with wicked fists. You cannot fast as you do today and expect your voice to be heard on high. Is this the kind of fast I have chosen, only a day for people to humble themselves? Is it only for bowing one's head like a reed and for lying in sackcloth and ashes? Is that what you call a fast, a day acceptable to the LORD?

Is not this the kind of fasting I have chosen: to loose the chains of injustice and untie the cords of the yoke, to set the oppressed free and break every yoke? Is it not to share your food with the hungry and to provide the poor wanderer with shelter—when you see the naked, to clothe them, and not to turn away from your own flesh and blood? Then your light will break forth like the dawn, and your healing will quickly appear; then your righteousness will go before you, and the glory of the LORD will be your rear guard. Then you will call, and the LORD will answer; you will cry for help, and he will say: Here am I.

If you do away with the yoke of oppression, with the pointing finger and malicious talk, and if you spend yourselves in behalf of the hungry and satisfy the needs of the oppressed, then your light will rise in the darkness, and your night will become like the noonday. The LORD will guide you always;

he will satisfy your needs in a sun-scorched land and will strengthen your frame. You will be like a well-watered garden, like a spring whose waters never fail. Your people will rebuild the ancient ruins and will raise up the age-old foundations; you will be called Repairer of Broken Walls, Restorer of Streets with Dwellings.

If you keep your feet from breaking the Sabbath and from doing as you please on my holy day, if you call the Sabbath a delight and the LORD's holy day honorable, and if you honor it by not going your own way and not doing as you please or speaking idle words, then you will find your joy in the LORD, and I will cause you to ride in triumph on the heights of the land and to feast on the inheritance of your father Jacob."

For the mouth of the LORD has spoken. (Isa. 58:1–14)

As you read these passages, perhaps you noticed a familiar theme: God focused on the Israelites' *lack* of doing. Though the Israelites had been going through the religious motions, they had been over-looking people who were near and dear to the heart of God—people like the hungry, the disenfranchised, the marginalized, and the poor. God specifically mentioned the lack of concern and care for widows and orphans.

As you study these passages and others, it becomes clear that it's possible to live a very religious life—even avoiding the things on the Thou Shall Not lists—and still fall short of fulfilling God's mission and purpose. Therefore, being holy, or reflecting the nature and character of God, is not just about avoiding certain behaviors that are called sin. It is very much about doing certain things. In other words, the Christian life is far less about passivity than it is about activity. This call from a passive faith to a faith defined by activity is simply a reflection of the nature and character of God.

ACTIVE GOD

There is much that people can disagree on about the nature and character of God, but on this one truth, there isn't much room for debate: God is not a passive God. If He were, I would not be here now, and you would not be wherever you are now. If God were passive, not only would you and I not exist, but here would not exist and neither would there. Confused yet? This is what I am saying: if God were passive, creation would never have taken place. If God were passive in nature, He would have been content to exist all alone for the expanse of eternity while He sat on His throne, twiddling His thumbs. Our God is not a passive God. Quite the contrary—He is an active God. Our God has been, is, and will always be on the move.

So what? Why do I go out of my way to build the case that ours is an active God? Because living the Christian faith is about modeling the nature and character of God. And to model the nature and character of God, you first must understand Him.

If ours was a passive God, we wouldn't be entertaining questions about the nature of the Christian faith because there would be no Christian faith. The Christian faith required action to be taken by God. Not subtle action. Significant, breathtaking, life-offering action. The establishment of the Christian faith required the Father in heaven to *send* (verb) His only Son to *live* (verb) and *die* (verb) and *resurrect* (verb) for the sins of humanity. During His ministry, Jesus healed the sick, fed the hungry, pursued the outcasts of society, and invested in the overlooked and undervalued. Study the Gospels: Jesus was always on the move, from early in the morning until late at night. There is not a single moment in the gospel story where we find Jesus being passive. He was on the move, and He called people to do and to be the same.

Jesus came to establish a church that would be an extension of Himself. As His ministry began and He called His first followers, He immediately called them to action. Whenever He approached a potential disciple, we find Him speaking these two simple, yet incredibly profound words over and over: "Follow Me." Action was written into the DNA of Christianity from the moment the movement began. In fact, when people wanted to follow Him but didn't move quickly enough, Jesus explained that the kingdom was too urgent to wait. He told one guy to let the dead bury their own dead. Sounds rude, but the King and His kingdom were and are on the move, and there is no time to sit and wait.

Imagine how differently the Gospels would have played out if Jesus approached potential disciples and said, "Here is a list of things I want you to avoid doing." He would have developed a group of nice, safe, inactive people, and the church would have died before it was even fully established.

I suppose it is quite easy to look way back in history and acknowledge that God was quite active. If you flip through pages of the Old Testament, it's hard to deny it. However, it is not enough to acknowledge that God used to be on the move. Doing so suggests that the movement and action of God are a thing of the past, and now He has settled into cosmic retirement.

So perhaps He still desires action from His people, but He hasn't moved off the throne in a while.

While it is certainly noble to think about God ruling on His throne, nothing could be further from the truth than to also assume God is content to stay still.

God is still moving, perhaps more actively than ever before. Before Jesus ascended to heaven, He told His disciples that when He left, the Holy Spirit would come. Knowing the disciples would have done anything in their power to keep Jesus on earth, He explained that they were actually better off if He left them. From their perspective, how could that possibly be true? For three years they had spent every waking moment with Him. They had listened to Him teach, they'd had front-row seats to His miracles, they had benefited from His fishing advice—they had been with Him, with God, for three years … and now they were being told they would be better off when He left. They must have wondered how that could be.

And yet Jesus said in John 14:12, "Very truly I tell you, whoever believes in me will do the works I have been doing, and they will do even greater things than these, because I am going to the Father."

If I can take the liberty to paraphrase Jesus's words just a bit, He told them, "You think you have seen Me on the move? You think I have been active in this world? Wait until you see what happens when the Holy Spirit comes." What the disciples didn't understand was that, yes, Jesus is God, and yes, He was with them—but He was just one. But when the Holy Spirit of God came, He wouldn't just be *with* them; He would move *into* them. Jesus explained that not only would the Holy Spirit work through them, but He would work and move and act in and through every person who claimed Jesus as Lord and Savior. Jesus said, "Trust Me, when the Holy Spirit comes, it'll be like nothing you've ever seen."

As Jesus promised, after He returned to heaven, the Spirit came. Not only did He come, but He came with a vengeance. He came not to kick back and relax, but to be on the move in and through Christ's bride, the church. And move He did. If you study the book of Acts, you will find that what began as a few believers sitting in a small upper room quickly multiplied into thousands of believers. What began as one small church in one small corner of the Roman Empire quickly became hundreds of churches scattered throughout every nook and cranny of the empire.

In Acts 17, not long after the Spirit came, one of the political leaders of the day accused the church of turning the world upside down in the name of Jesus. Though they were guilty as charged, the real perpetrator was the Spirit, who had been doing in and through them just what He came to do: move. And in Acts 17, the movement of the Spirit had only just begun. His plan now is the same as it was then—to continue turning the world upside down in the name of Jesus.

GRAFFITI FAITH

I am not a big fan of gas station bathrooms. I know—crazy, right? Between the filth and the aroma, gas station bathrooms are nothing more and nothing less than a necessary evil in my life. When I do have to use such a facility, I do so as quickly and as cleanly as possible. But apparently, there are some others who don't mind lingering in gas station bathrooms a bit longer. Almost always, words or images are etched into the walls of the stalls. I avoid spending much time studying these artistic expressions—some of them would make Howard Stern blush—but I have read and seen my fair share. The vast majority of the scrawling simply says, "So-and-so was here."

In a sense, as Christians we have been called to leave graffiti marks on the paths we walk and live. The way we live, the way we love, should leave an etching that simply says, "God was here." This whole idea may seem strange, like a figment of my twisted imagination, but it's actually derived from the prayer Jesus taught us to pray.

Growing up in the Jewish culture, Jesus's disciples had seen and prayed thousands of prayers. They were familiar with the Shema, which Jews prayed multiple times each day.

But there must have been something distinctly different about the way Jesus prayed, because at one point early in His ministry, the disciples approached Him and said, "Lord, teach us to pray" (Luke 11:1). Undoubtedly, Jesus was eager to teach them how to pray effectively—He knew better than anyone else the great power that is wrapped up in prayer.

According to Matthew's gospel, the prayer Jesus taught them went like this:

> Our Father in heaven,
> hallowed be your name,
> your kingdom come,

> your will be done,
> on earth as it is in heaven.
> Give us today our daily bread.
> And forgive us our debts,
> as we also have forgiven our debtors.
> And lead us not into temptation,
> but deliver us from the evil one.

(Matt. 6:9–13)

There is so much that could be said about this prayer, but I want to focus on one line in particular that may be more misunderstood than all the others.

Your will be done, on earth as it is in heaven.

Christians have recited this prayer for hundreds of years now—oftentimes in a corporate setting, other times in silence and solitude. Regardless of the setting or the language in which this prayer is uttered, it is all too often prayed with a false perspective in mind. Too many times Christians have spoken this portion of the Lord's Prayer with a voice of passivity. In other words, "Hey, God, this is Your world; You do what You want done. I am not going to get in Your way or hinder Your work. In fact, I am going to cheer You on as You carry out Your work and Your will."

Perhaps, at first reading, you see nothing wrong with this para-phrase. I know I have prayed this way at times. Undoubtedly we choose this passive approach with the very best of intentions, but when this prayer is prayed in such a way, something has gone terribly wrong. "Your will be done, on earth as it is in heaven" is not a line you can just mumble as you roll out of bed or as you stand in pew three of your local church while dressed to the nines. No, quite the contrary: we can voice this prayer appropriately only when our sleeves are rolled up and our hands are ready to move. This prayer is not intended to say, "Hey, God, do what You do—I am all for it." Instead, this prayer is intended to be, "God, use me to do what You want done—I am all in." When you mouth these words, you are inviting God to unleash Himself in you and through you and around you. This is a dangerous prayer, but a necessary one. God intends for His people to offer a glimpse of heaven on earth, and the very way we offer a glimpse of heaven on earth is by carrying out God's will on earth as it is in heaven.

I like to think about it this way: anywhere a Christian works or sits or stands or worships or plays, heaven and earth should overlap. The way we live our lives within our circles of influence should forever be etching not "God was here" but "God is here."

When you believe in a passive God, faith in Him is safe, predictable, and harmless both to you and others. However, when you believe in an active God, a God who is on the move and expects you to be as well, then suddenly penny loafers and pressed slacks are no longer the appropriate attire—you need to put on your fire suit and crash helmet.

Yes, God was active.

But more importantly, God *is* active.

He is not stagnant; He is moving, so we should be too.

Moral compliance is hugely significant, but we cannot settle for a passive faith defined simply by avoiding certain behaviors. If God is an active God—and He is—then why would He institute a passive faith?

He wouldn't.

He didn't.

The faith of the Bible is defined by action.

SINS OF OMISSION

Now, I know you might find yourself getting antsy in your seat as you read because you just might think I'm saying Christianity is all about works. The faith versus works debate has raged on for centuries and will continue to do so without my involvement. Nothing I write is intended to suggest that the Christian life is primarily about external works—because our doing flows from our being. As James said, "Faith without works is dead" (2:20 KJV). Truly placing your faith in an active God will naturally result in an active faith.

The sins I believe are most prevalent in the church today may not show up on the radar of some church leadership, and they rarely are included in research studies. But they are directly related to the mission and purpose God has for our lives. Undoubtedly, sin is sin is sin, but I do think some sins are more dangerous than others. And the most dangerous sins are the ones that go unnoticed.

There is no question that in the landscape of Christianity today, there are significant visible, active sin issues. Gossip, slander, homosexuality, drug addiction … the list could go on and on. All of these sins of commission and many others are real and they are dangerous, but in my opinion, the most dangerous sins are the sins of omission. Sins of omission are not a result of activity but of inactivity. As James

4:17 says, "If anyone, then, knows the good they ought to do and doesn't do it, it is sin for them."

Sins of omission are actions God has called us to that we fail to live out. Perhaps the actions feel a bit too radical, or unsafe, or irresponsible—and yet God has called us nonetheless. Yes, He has placed some restrictions in our lives, and when we break, ignore, or overlook those restrictions, we are guilty of sin. But as I study the heart of God in the Scriptures, I believe the major sins that silently lurk in the lives of many Christians are the sins of omission. Perhaps we have placed too much emphasis on the Thou Shall Nots at the expense of the Thou Shalls.

In the next section, I have mapped out a blueprint for an active Christian faith. I have broken down a life of active faith into four categories, and each one of the categories is a verb. Each verb is built upon sometimes-overlooked scriptures that call us to action. We will discover along the way that the actions tucked away in these passages are not suggested by God but demanded by God. Now, I know *demanded* is a word that may feel a bit uncomfortable, but some discomfort may do us good. Some discomfort may get our hearts pounding, our palms sweating, and our muscles moving for the purpose of spreading God's glory and reflecting His nature and character in this world.

REFLECT & DISCUSS

1. This chapter opened with this idea: "There is an undeniable relationship between our under-standing of God and our expression of faith."

What does your expression of faith say about who you believe God to be and what you believe He is about?

2. Study Isaiah 1:10–17 and 58:1–14 again. Pay careful attention to the seemingly good religious activities the Israelites were carrying out, and yet notice God's displeasure. If God evaluated your faith in a similar way, how do you think He would respond?

3. The Christian life is far more about activity than passivity. As you evaluate your faith, how do you measure up with that statement? Is your faith primarily defined by certain things you no longer do? Or are you actively chasing after the heart of God?

4. God is active. Spend some time in Scripture, taking notice of the movement of God. Does He seem to be on the move in your faith community? In you? Why? Why not?

5. As you think about sins of commission and sins of omission, which seem to be a bigger issue in your life and faith? Why? Be specific.

PRAYER

Father, I know You are a God on the move. You always have been, and You always will be. My faith should model Your same passion and movement. Forgive me for the ways I have settled for faith defined by passivity—sometimes at the expense of godly activity. Transform my heart to be like Yours: a heart that beats for those who live outside the margins. May Your will be done on earth as it is in heaven. When I say those words, I am not simply encouraging You to do what You do best, but inviting You to do what You do best in and through and for me. Comfortable or not. Safe or not. Predictable or not. Use me to turn this community, region, and world upside down again. As I continue on this journey of rediscovery, I ask You to move not just my heart but my muscles too, in the name of Jesus and on behalf of Jesus. In Jesus's name.

Part II

MOVING BEYOND THE NOTS

Chapter 3

GO

Familiarity can be a problem.

I fly on a regular basis—regionally, nationally, and internationally. Sometimes the flight is overbooked; other times I get a row to myself. Sometimes the plane is equipped with individual TV screens for every seat; other times there is not even one screen for everyone to share. Sometimes the meals are tasty, and … I just caught myself in a fib.

There is one constant on every flight, though: the safety speech prior to takeoff. You probably know the scene. The flight attendant stands positioned in the center of the aisle, ready to deliver the spiel. For some reason, though the planes are state of the art, the audio equipment usually is not, and so the flight attendant uses a push-button walkie-talkie device. For a minute or so the flight attendant thoroughly explains the safety equipment on the plane and how to utilize the equipment in case of an emergency. My favorite part is when they show how to fasten a seat belt; I suppose that is for the people on board who have not been in an automobile at any point during the last fifty years.

As the flight attendant assumes position to begin the speech, most passengers also assume a certain position: eyes rolling, shoulders shrugging. They pay attention to anything but the lifesaving information being shared.

Familiarity is the problem. Most passengers would claim they do not need to pay serious attention to the safety instructions because they are so familiar with them. They could recite the words. And of course, in a life-and-death situation they could live out the words.

But is that really true?

I am included in the "most passengers" category. Though I have heard the safety speech hundreds of times, I really have very little idea what is actually said. If I ever find myself in a life-and-death situation aboard a plane, I will likely be in real trouble. Where is the flotation device again? How do I get the oxygen running through the tube? Where are the exits?

The problem is not with the supposedly familiar instructions; the problem is with the supposed familiarity with the instructions.

GREAT COMMISSION CONFUSION

> Then Jesus came to them and said, "All authority in heaven and on earth has been given to me. Therefore go and make disciples of all nations, baptizing them in the name of the Father and of the Son and of the Holy Spirit, and teaching them to obey everything I have commanded you. And surely I am with you always, to the very end of the age." (Matt. 28:18–20)

There are endless ways this command from Jesus could be dissected, but here is the bottom line of Jesus's command: go and multiply yourselves. We could diagram the logic of this passage, unpack the original language, and talk about the historical background, but all of that complex work can be simplified back down to this: you are followers of Jesus; go make more followers of Jesus.

If you have been following Jesus for a while, then the command to Go is very possibly like the safety-information speech prior to takeoff. *Yeah, yeah, yeah. I know. I get it.* You have likely seen the words written and heard them taught—perhaps you can even recite them from memory. You are familiar with the instructions. And maybe you have even found yourself tempted to skip over this chapter because you are familiar with the same old spiel.

But there is a problem. Jesus's command paints a picture of disciples making disciples making disciples making disciples. Disciples making disciples making disciples equates to explosive growth, quite contrary to the current pattern of growth in the American church. George Barna Online Research states that fifty to seventy-five churches every week close their doors for the last time.[1] They sing their last song, plan their last worship service, share their last potluck meal, and then lock the doors for the last time. There are numerous factors contributing to this reality, but the core issue is not something that is happening, but something that is not happening.

The instructions are not being heeded. Going is not happening.

There is a problem.

However the problem is not with the supposedly familiar instructions; the problem is with the supposed familiarity with the instructions.

Familiarity does not equal clarity. Instead, confusion can coexist quite easily with familiarity. Just like I can hear the safety spiel on a plane hundreds of times and still wrestle with basic questions like, "Where is the flotation device? How do I get the oxygen flowing? Where are the emergency exits?" the command to Go can be heard over and over again while still leaving more confusion than clarity. Not only *can* confusion still exist in the midst of familiarity, but when it comes to the Great Commission, confusion *does* exist. So let me address three commonly accepted ideas about the Great Commission. Each represents confusion, and each explains why the mission has not yet been completed.

GOING IS AN EVENT

I'll never forget the time Billy Graham and I crossed paths. Well, sort of. Well, not really at all. What I mean is that I will never forget the time I was visiting the city of Cincinnati at the same time Billy Graham was holding a crusade. I was not even attending the crusade but I still felt the effects. There was a buzz in the air; traffic was heavy. More than seventy thousand people were pouring into downtown Cincinnati to experience the event. Thousands undoubtedly turned to Jesus as Lord and Savior.

In terms of the Great Commission, I think many people think about Going primarily as an event. Perhaps the event is a packed stadium where the gospel is preached. Perhaps the event is a spring-break mission trip to a third-world country or a good old-fashioned tent revival or a special door-to-door initiative in your community the weekend before Easter.

Such events certainly play a role in Going, and yet, honestly, they play a small part, because they are isolated.

When Jesus gave the instruction to Go, He was not thinking in terms of events; He was thinking about our lifestyle.

Go could be better understood in this way: "as you are going."

Viewing the Go command from this perspective is a game changer—and more so a life changer. Not just for you, but for others.

When Go is viewed as a daily mission, not a scheduled event or activity, a sense of awareness is heightened and opportunity abounds. Whether you are a successful professional, a graduate student, a retiree, a trainee, a senior citizen, or a senior in high school … you are going. There is no question about whether you are going—you are, and so am I.

Everyone, everywhere is going. Always.

The question changes, then, from whether you are going to whether you are fulfilling the mission as you are going.

In Acts 1:7–8, Jesus used very specific language in regard to our mission.

> It is not for you to know the times or dates the
> Father has set by his own authority. But you will
> receive power when the Holy Spirit comes on you;
> and you will be my witnesses in Jerusalem, and in
> all Judea and Samaria, and to the ends of the earth.

I find Jesus's choice of words interesting. He didn't say we are to be theologians here, there, and everywhere. He didn't say we need to spread religion here, there, and everywhere. Jesus said, "Be my witnesses." The word *witness* is a familiar one; it derives from a court-room setting. During a trial, witnesses will be called to the stand to testify under oath, and they will be asked to testify about what or whom they have seen or heard. So, if you were a witness to an accident, you would be asked to describe in the greatest possible detail how the accident occurred and perhaps who was at fault. And if you were a witness to a crime, you may be asked to recount the sights and sounds you observed as the crime took place. Very simply, a witness is someone who testifies about what he or she has seen or heard.

Jesus said, "You will be my witnesses." So, are you? Do you? On a regular basis do you find yourself sharing with others about what you have seen and heard Jesus do? Using witness language really simplifies the mission we have been given. Many people overcomplicate the gospel message and the qualifications needed to share the good news. A seminary degree may be helpful, but it's not necessary to be a witness. Impressive letters before and after your name may increase your vocational opportunities, but they are not necessary to be a witness. The ability to read and understand the original biblical languages is impressive, but it is not necessary to serve as a witness.

For evidence of this truth, we need look no further than the scene where Jesus first gave the Go command. He was gathered on a mountaintop with a group of ragtag fishermen—also known as His first disciples—and He was preparing to ascend into heaven.

He explained to them—and I am paraphrasing—"From now on you will be My witnesses." In other words, "I will no longer be here in person, so you are responsible to testify about what you have seen and heard." Jesus had been on the earth for around thirty-three years, which included a three-year ministry, and now He was leaving.

In doing so He gave His followers the responsibility to share the message about His life and death and resurrection with the entire known world. The men who only three years before had been fishing and collecting taxes were responsible to take the message of Jesus to the ends of the earth. In his book *The Jesus I Never Knew*, Philip Yancey wrote, "By ascending, Jesus took the risk of being forgotten."[2] Essentially Jesus left it up to a small inner circle of His followers to make sure that He wasn't forgotten. Can you imagine how overwhelmed and unqualified for the task they must have felt? They had no formal theological training, no impressive degrees. They didn't have awe-inspiring spiritual résumés; very likely they didn't feel qualified to carry out the task they had been given.

Isn't it true that many of us feel the same way they must have felt? Overwhelmed and unqualified? The difficult part of witnessing is not identifying people who need to have Jesus in their lives; it is knowing how to share the news of Jesus.

As a pastor I have had many people explain to me how they would like to share Jesus with other people, but they are unsure of what to say. More times than I can count, I have heard, "I just don't feel like I know enough to share with other people." I understand that, and the corporate church certainly has the responsibility to work toward equipping people with appropriate knowledge. However, a lack of knowledge is no justification to excuse yourself from sharing the message of Jesus. I always like to look at the issue this way: if you knew enough to decide to follow Jesus, then you know enough to invite someone else to follow Him. Perhaps that sounds simplistic, but it really should be that simple. As Christians we can so easily overcomplicate what it means to be Jesus's witnesses. The people I have known who have been the most effective witnesses for Christ do not have any fancy titles before or after their names, and they do not have diplomas from impressive seminaries hanging on their walls. They are simply those who tell the story of what Jesus has done in their lives.

One of the most effective evangelists in the New Testament was an unsuspecting person whose story we learn about in John 4. As Jesus was passing through Samaria, He encountered a Samaritan woman who had come to draw water from a well.

Now, we know some things about her simply by the fact that she was at the well at midday. In those days the women would usually travel together in the earliest hours of the morning to draw water together so they could avoid the hottest part of the day. So the fact that this woman was at the well during the day, alone, was an obvious cultural indication that she was living on the margins of society. And there was a good reason why she was living as an outcast. John 4 tells us the woman had had five husbands and was now living with another man who was not her husband. She was probably the talk of the town, but not in a good way. When she walked down the street, everyone else would have moved to the other side. When she walked into a restaurant, all the people there would have called for their checks and left.

But then she encountered Jesus.

Jesus said to the woman, "Will you give me a drink?" (John 4:7). Now, if you don't know any better, this seems like a very unassuming question. But culturally, this was a barrier-shattering question for at least two reasons. First, a good Jew would never willingly associate with a Samaritan. Jewish people considered Samaritans to be half-breeds at best and something less than human at worst. The Jews hated the Samaritans, and from the perspective of the Samaritans, the feeling was mutual. The Jews so despised Samaritans that, whenever possible, they would avoid even traveling through Samaria. Instead, they would take a well-worn path that went around Samaria. A Jew would never associate with a Samaritan, and a Jewish man would never speak to a woman in public. But in John 4 we find Jesus talking to a Samaritan woman. The woman was shocked. In fact verse 9 tells us, "The Samaritan woman said to him, 'You are a Jew and I am a Samaritan woman. How can you ask me for a drink?'"

Jesus responded, "If you knew the gift of God and who it is that asks you for a drink, you would have asked him and he would have given you living water" (v. 10). As the conversation played out, the woman was perplexed: she thought Jesus was talking about physical water when in reality He was speaking in spiritual terms. But Jesus had promised that He could offer water that would quench her thirst forever, so she said, "'Sir, give me this water so that I won't get thirsty and have to keep coming here to draw water.'

"He told her, 'Go, call your husband and come back.'

'I have no husband,' she replied.

"Jesus said to her, 'You are right when you say you have no husband. The fact is, you have had five husbands, and the man you now have is not your husband. What you have just said is quite true'" (vv. 15–18).

Very quickly the Samaritan woman realized the man she was talking to was not just an ordinary man. In fact, in the midst of the conversation, Jesus identified himself as the Messiah. After the conversation ended, the disciples returned from town and the woman returned back to town. Interestingly, she left her water jug behind.

She traveled to the well to draw water to survive for the day, and yet she was so captivated by her experience with Jesus that she left the water behind. She came to the well physically thirsty and left the well spiritually quenched. When she traveled back into the town, she told anyone who would listen about her experience. You would expect that because she was an outsider and had no influence, no one would have listened to her, and yet verse 39 says, "Many of the Samaritans from that town believed in him because of the woman's testimony, 'He told me everything I ever did.'"

Some translations say that as a result of her testimony, the whole town went out to meet Jesus and many believed. If a woman living on the bottom rung of society can share Jesus with a whole town of people, what is your excuse? What is my excuse?

Here is what you cannot miss: the Samaritan woman was not successful as an evangelist because she was an expert in the Old Testament law or because she was an eloquent communicator, but simply because she was Jesus's witness, and she testified about what He did in her life.

One of the most effective ways to be Jesus's witness to others is to share the story of what He has done in your life.

You could tell how Jesus rescued you from the depths of addiction, or how He redeemed a past that was checkered with criminal behavior. Such stories are incredibly effective, and I encourage you to share them anytime there is the opportunity.

But quite possibly you do not even feel like you have a story to tell about how Jesus has worked in your life. Perhaps you have been in church since the first Sunday out of the womb, you cannot remember a time when you didn't believe in God, and you have had

John 3:16 memorized since the time you learned to talk. Maybe the details of your life are a bit different, but I know there are many people who don't really feel like they have a testimony to share. We tend to think that testimonies have to be flashy or full of shocking details, but the truth is that if you are a follower of Jesus, you have a testimony. Not only do you have a testimony of what Jesus has done in your life, but—whether you realize it or not—you have an incredibly powerful, earth-shattering testimony that has unleashed a raging river of implication coursing through heaven and hell. If you are a follower of Jesus, you have a captivating testimony even if you do not feel like you do.

The apostle Paul communicated our story as Christians this way:

> As for you, you were dead in your transgressions and sins, in which you used to live when you followed the ways of this world and of the ruler of the kingdom of the air, the spirit who is now at work in those who are disobedient. All of us also lived among them at one time, gratifying the cravings of our flesh and following its desires and thoughts. Like the rest, we were by nature deserving of wrath. But because of his great love for us, God, who is rich in mercy, made us alive with Christ even when we were dead in transgressions—it is by grace you have been saved. (Eph. 2:1–5)

No matter what the other details of your story may be, it begins this way: "I was dead, but because of Jesus, now I am alive." That is a pretty captivating story about what you have seen and heard and experienced of Jesus.

Going is not an event but a lifestyle. As you are going, serve as a witness.

As you go to work Monday through Friday from eight until five, don't just trade your time for money; use the time as an opportunity to be a witness for Jesus.

As you go to school year after year, study hard and learn a lot, along the way serve as a witness for Jesus.

After you have retired, don't settle for kicking back and coasting through the last couple of decades of life; be intentional about continuing to build new relationships so you can serve as a witness for Jesus.

And if you are a stay-at-home parent, don't feel like you are exempt from being a witness; you have children who listen to every word you say and are watching your every move. You have a captive audience; as you are going through your day, be a witness for Jesus.

Going is a lifestyle defined by witnessing about what you have seen and heard Jesus do, not just in your life, but also in the lives of others.

GOING IS AN OPTION

I have often heard people attempt to rationalize their lack of participation in the Great Commission by explaining that witnessing is just not a gift they have been given. Well-meaning people often use 1 Corinthians 12:27–30 as the trump card to justify their personal lack of participation in the mission:

> Now you are the body of Christ, and each one
> of you is a part of it. And God has placed in the
> church first of all apostles, second prophets, third
> teachers, then miracles, then gifts of healing, of
> helping, of guidance, and of different kinds of
> tongues. Are all apostles? Are all prophets? Are all
> teachers? Do all work miracles? Do all have gifts of
> healing? Do all speak in tongues? Do all interpret?

According to that passage, teaching is labeled as a gift. That verse seems to open the door for some people to excuse themselves from the mission because only *some* have the gift of teaching. Therefore, if you are not one of the *some*, you get a free pass. Now, there are very few who would actually articulate such an argument, but I also believe that mind-set is alive and well, and the quoted passage seems to justify it.

However, it does not. Are there some who are especially gifted as teachers and preachers? Of course. But does the absence of the ability to communicate the gospel to hundreds or thousands at a time serve as a valid reason to excuse oneself from the mission? Of course not.

Serving as a witness is not an option; it's an obligation.

Perhaps the word *obligation* used in this context made you wince a bit, and understandably so. *Obligation* tends to carry a negative connotation. We are quick to think about certain aspects of life in terms of obligation: paying taxes, taking out the trash, and tasting our mother-in-law's newest recipes. Obligations do not typically stir up warm and fuzzy feelings. In fact, many people would prefer to avoid the obligations of life, not embrace them.

When I label serving as a witness as an "obligation," I am not thinking about the connotation we usually attach to the word. *Obligation* in this context is a "get to," not a "have to."

Almost nine years ago I willingly obliged myself to someone. In front of my friends and family, I sealed my promise to my bride with the words "I do." When I said, "I do," I obliged myself to care for her in sickness and in health, in poverty and in wealth, in good times and in bad, until death do us part.

I am obligated to her, but this is a "get to" obligation. Yes, I'm obligated to spend the rest of my life with my wife, but there is nothing else I would rather do.

Some obligations are not burdens, but opportunities you wouldn't forego for anything.

In John 5 we read about a man who had been crippled for thirty-eight years. He lay beside the Pool of Bethesda, a place where the lame, the blind, and the crippled gathered because people believed that when the water was stirred, it could heal. Because of his condition, this man had never made it into the water, and so when Jesus encountered him, He asked, "Do you want to get well?" (v. 6). Perhaps Jesus asked that question tongue in cheek, because of course the man wanted to be well. The man told Jesus, "I have no one to help me into the pool when the water is stirred. While I am trying to get in, someone else goes down ahead of me" (v. 7). Jesus simply looked at him and said, "Pick up your mat and walk" (v. 8). And at once the man was healed. The Bible doesn't say so, but I would guess he began hopping and skipping and jumping as he experienced flexibility and strength in his limbs, and surely he was shouting at the top of his lungs all the while. We are told very few details about this man's life, but I love the way his story ends: "The man went away and told the Jewish leaders that it was Jesus who had made him well" (v. 15).

The crippled man was healed, and instantly he felt obliged to tell everyone everywhere the good news. Wouldn't you?

Interestingly, the same Greek word used in the New Testament for salvation also means "healing." And so if you are a follower of Jesus, this is another way to tell your story: "Jesus has made me well."

Several years ago, the once famous (now infamous) athlete Lance Armstrong was interviewed about his tireless efforts to raise funds for and awareness about cancer research. During the interview he explained his motivation this way: "I guess it's the obligation of the cured."[3]

Serving as a witness for Jesus is not an option. It's an obligation: the obligation of the cured.

When you truly understand you have been healed—not just of cancer, like Lance was, but of sin—telling others the story of what Jesus has done is not a "have to" but a "get to." Not an option but an obligation.

GOING IS ABOUT PLACES

When most people think about Going, they think in terms of geography: places. And so many people would say they would be all about fulfilling the Go mission if only they had the opportunity to go. If they had the time or resources to visit a distant land or an impoverished country or to cross a border, then they would be busy about the command to Go. There is an if/then mentality that can easily develop in this regard. *If I could only Go to _____, then ...*

But what if the Great Commission isn't about geography at all?

Now certainly, as Jesus explained the mission of the church to His closest followers, geography was a part of the conversation. In Acts 1:7–8 Jesus said, "It is not for you to know the times or dates the Father has set by his own authority. But you will receive power when the Holy Spirit comes on you; and you will be my witnesses in Jerusalem, and in all Judea and Samaria, and to the ends of the earth."

Clearly, Jesus spoke in geographical terms, but even then His mind was filled with the names and faces of men, women, and children from every tribe, tongue, and nation. So of course, some Christians, perhaps even many, need to get passports and go through customs and fly over water if the Great Commission is going to be completed. But some of us also need to stay. The bottom line is this: all of us are called to Go even if we stay.

If you studied the entire book of Acts, you would find that the expansion of the church followed the model Jesus laid out. The first seven chapters describe the impact of the gospel in Jerusalem. Then, Acts 8–12 depicts the impact of the gospel in several places in Judea and Samaria. Acts 13–28 highlights the spread of the gospel to major cities throughout the whole Roman Empire, which at the time was the known civilized world.

Though going places—even distant places—is certainly integral to fulfilling the mission, thinking primarily in terms of geography does not fully encompass what Jesus was up to, and it offers too many Christians a free pass not to participate.

Somehow the Great Commission has become an assignment for certain people in the church—usually those who have a passion about international missions. And if participating in or carrying out the Great Commission implies traveling to or living in a foreign land, then just on a very practical level, most Christians are given a free pass to sit back and passively observe.

If the Great Commission is primarily about geography, then very few people will feel compelled to be involved in the work. Sure, they may send a check or two throughout the year to help finance the work of those who are participating in the Great Commission, but the efforts will likely stop there. Honestly, if the Great Commission is reduced to only distant geographical locations, then I understand the disconnection that seems to have taken place in the hearts and minds of so many Christians.

But what if the Great Commission is not about times zones but about men, women, and children? What if the emphasis is not on cities but on souls?

What if the Great Commission is simply about names and faces?

If the Great Commission is about names and faces—and it is—then there are no more free passes to avoid participation. The if/then mentality gets replaced by a right-here, right-now mentality. Christians do not need to wait for the opportunity to Go to a certain place to be on mission; the mission begins "here," wherever your "here" may be.

The Great Commission is about names and faces.

In your community.

In your neighborhood.

In your school.

In your office.

In your living room.

Hopefully you will have opportunities to Go "there" to help complete the mission, but in the meantime, be on mission "here."

Going is not an event but a lifestyle.

Going is not an option but an obligation.

Going is not about places but about people.

These principles each represent elements of common confusion, even in the midst of the familiarity with Jesus's command to Go. Yet the core issue hindering the mission is something much deeper and more serious.

The sense of familiarity has eliminated a sense of urgency.

You have probably heard Aesop's fable *The Boy Who Cried Wolf* about the little boy who cried out for help because of a wolf too many times when there was no wolf in sight. And in the end, when a wolf really arrived, the boy cried wolf, but no one heeded the warning. He had cried wolf one too many times.

In some scenarios, familiarity reduces a sense of urgency.

When the flight attendant shares the safety speech, there should be eerie music playing in the background because the scenario described is one of life and death. But because the information is familiar, people treat the message as anything but urgent.

The same thing has happened with the command to Go. It is literally a matter of life and death for millions of men, women, and children, yet many of us settle in and tune out Jesus's call to Go. The message is urgent, but in many ways our response to the message would suggest it is anything but.

Your sense of urgency in regard to the Go command will be in direct proportion to the way you view people.

When I walk into the grocery store or post office in my community, I often notice the bulletin board that is covered with the faces of missing children. Occasionally I will pause for a moment or two to take a closer look, but after a brief hesitation, I'll continue on my way to buy the milk or bread or mail a letter or two. My guess is that you respond in the same way. Perhaps you give casual interest, but not much more. However, imagine how differently the scenario would play out if your child was missing. Each time you passed a bulletin board with missing persons on it, your eyes would hungrily devour the faces, ensuring your child's picture was on display. Not only that, but you would also run and shout and flail your arms, doing whatever necessary to share a photo with anyone and everyone in sight. All day. Every day. In the relentless pursuit to find your child, the amount of necessary resources would be irrelevant; any kind of concern about how people perceive your actions and words would be nonexistent, and complacency would have no place in your life. Instead, urgency would be your constant companion.

When Jesus said "Go," He wasn't sending us on a mission to seek and save a nameless, faceless crowd. He sent us to save children—not someone else's children, but His children. I like to envision that the walls of heaven are covered from floor to ceiling with names and faces of men, women, and children from every tribe, every tongue, every nation—and that all of them have these two things in common: they are children of God, and they are lost. And every time a person is found and enters into a relationship with Jesus, a picture is pulled down from the wall and shredded into confetti … and the party begins.

In Luke 15:10 Jesus said, "I tell you, there is rejoicing in the presence of the angels of God over one sinner who repents."

Go is not a suggestion but a command. Not about religion but about relationship. Not about a crowd but about children.

The instruction to Go may be familiar, but it couldn't be more urgent.

"Therefore Go and make disciples ..."

Are you?

Will you?

When?

REFLECT & DISCUSS

1. If you are honest, are you serving as a witness "as you are going"? Do you find yourself regularly sharing with others about what you have seen and heard Jesus doing?

2. If you are not actively sharing Jesus with others, what do you believe is the most significant obstacle? Lack of knowledge? Lack of opportunity? Lack of courage? Discuss practical ways to overcome these apparent obstacles.

3. Reflect on the story of how you began a relationship with Jesus. Now think about how to share your story with others in a meaningful way.

4. Ultimately, Going is about names and faces. Take some time to list people within your circle of influence with whom you can intentionally share Jesus. If you have trouble thinking of the names and faces, answer these questions: Whose numbers are programmed into your cell phone?

Who lives next door to you on both sides and across the street? Who do you report to on the organizational chart at work? Who reports to you? Who lives in your house?

If you answer these questions, you will likely develop a list of people within your circle of influence. Now Go, tell, share, and make disciples.

PRAYER

Father, You have sent me on Your behalf to make disciples of all nations. Whether I am nudged to another time zone or simply across the street, give me courage, boldness, and willingness to be a witness for You. In times when I feel overwhelmed and underqualified for the task and by the task, remind me that I am not alone and that I am capable. Stir me up and remind me of the great urgency in regard to this task. Children are lost—Your children. Let me live with an appropriate level of energy and urgency. In Jesus's name.

Chapter 4

ACT

From the Mayans to Nostradamus to the latest religious leaders who are off their rockers, people have always loved making predictions about the end of time. They've made movies, created television series, and written books about it. And on almost a yearly basis, someone makes a bold prediction about the day the world will end.

According to the Mayan calendar, December 21, 2012, was the day the world was going to end. Now, I am no expert in the field, but according to my research, that prediction was wrong. Undoubtedly more predictions will be made in another year's time, and no matter how outlandish the predictions are, some people will take them seriously and rush to the grocery store to stock up on water.

Here is the reality: predictions will come and go, but no one knows when the final day will be. In fact, all of the people who have ever made a prediction about the end of the world have this one thing in common: they were wrong. The Bible says that no one knows the day or the hour when Jesus will return again, bringing time as we know it to a screeching halt. Even when Jesus was on earth, He claimed not to know the time of His return—only the Father does. From a Christian perspective, there's no *if* about judgment day and the end of the world. The only question is *when*.

> When the Son of Man comes in his glory, and all the angels with him, he will sit on his glorious throne. All the nations will be gathered before him, and he will separate the people one from another as a shepherd separates the sheep from the goats. He will put the sheep on his right and the goats on his left.
>
> Then the King will say to those on his right, "Come, you who are blessed by my Father; take your inheritance, the kingdom prepared for you since the creation of the world. For I was hungry and you gave me something to eat, I was thirsty and you gave me something to drink, I was a stranger and you invited me in, I needed clothes and you clothed me, I was sick and you looked after me, I was in prison and you came to visit me."
>
> Then the righteous will answer him, "Lord, when did we see you hungry and feed you, or thirsty and give you something to drink? When did we see you a stranger and invite you in, or needing clothes and clothe you? When did we see you sick or in prison and go to visit you?"
>
> The King will reply, "Truly I tell you, whatever you did for one of the least of these brothers and sisters of mine, you did for me."

Then he will say to those on his left, "Depart
from me, you who are cursed, into the eternal fire
prepared for the devil and his angels. For I was hungry and you gave me nothing to eat, I was thirsty
and you gave me nothing to drink, I was a stranger
and you did not invite me in, I needed clothes and
you did not clothe me, I was sick and in prison and
you did not look after me."

They also will answer, "Lord, when did we
see you hungry or thirsty or a stranger or needing
clothes or sick or in prison, and did not help you?"

He will reply, "Truly I tell you, whatever you
did not do for one of the least of these, you did not
do for me."

Then they will go away to eternal punishment,
but the righteous to eternal life. (Matt. 25:31–46)

I would suggest that while this is one of the most familiar passages in the New Testament, it is also one of the most misunderstood.
When studying this passage, many Christians smile and nod, but I
am not sure that's the most appropriate response if you truly understand what Jesus is saying. We should really break out in a cold sweat
about the reality of an impending judgment day.

As a Christian, you might be tempted to automatically categorize yourself as one of the righteous ones, or as a sheep. In life in
general we tend to overestimate ourselves, and so naturally we would
associate ourselves with the most honorable or comfortable category.
I don't know any Christians who would read this parable and label

themselves as goats. Usually I am not inclined to compare myself to sheep—they are dumb and smelly—but in the context of Matthew 25, being a sheep is the way to go.

Christians may also be quick to miss the intensity of this text because we assume that when Jesus is separating sheep from goats He is essentially separating churchgoers from nonchurchgoers. If that is what Jesus is doing in this parable, then indeed we are safe in skimming through this passage with little attention. But Jesus is not separating churchgoers from nonchurchgoers—He is not even separating self-proclaimed Jesus followers from everyone else.

One easy-to-miss word in this passage exposes what is really taking place. *Lord.* If you read the passage again, you will notice that the sheep and the goats both refer to Jesus as Lord.

When Jesus separates the sheep from the goats in Matthew 25, He is separating apparent Christians from apparent Christians. All of the people represented in this story are probably Sunday-morning churchgoers. They own Bibles, they may put money in the offering plate, they know the words to the songs—but according to this passage, some will spend eternity suffering in hell, while others will spend eternity in heaven.

Suddenly Matthew 25 doesn't seem like a passage to have your grandma knit into a pillow. Matthew 25 paints a picture of lifelong self-proclaimed Christians being separated from God for all of eternity. These are people who go to your church and sit in your pew and volunteer next to you.

One of these people may be you.

The reality is, on that day of judgment, Jesus will draw a line between those who have lived out His mission and purpose for their lives and those who haven't. According to Jesus, a factor that will determine which side of the line you will be on is whether or not you were compassionate.

Here is the struggle with compassion: almost everyone would say they are compassionate because of emotions they experience.

Maybe it is when you find yourself watching a Feed the Children documentary … a lump catches in your throat, and tears begin forming in the corners of your eyes …

Or when you notice someone begging on the side of the road, and as you drive away you get a knot in your stomach, thinking how desperate the person must feel …

Or when you hear stories about human trafficking that takes place locally and all around the globe, and you are overwhelmed with righteous anger and sadness …

Here is what we need to understand: from Jesus's perspective, compassion is not about emotion but motion. In Matthew 25, Jesus does not say, "You saw me thirsty and got sad," or, "You knew I was hungry and got a lump in your throat," or, "You saw I was without clothes and cried." No—Jesus speaks in terms of inactivity and activity because compassion is about action.

We could explain compassion in the following ways:

> Compassion is less about having a tear-stained face and more about having callused hands.
>
> Compassion is not about feeling sorry for people but advocating for people.
>
> Compassion is not about being disgusted by injustice but fighting injustice.

> Compassion is less about explaining poverty and
> more about alleviating poverty.

And so if we are going to take Jesus seriously, each of us has to take Matthew 25 as a template, hold it up against our lives, and ask ourselves, "Am I actively living out compassion?"

This is not a theoretical question but rather an extremely practical one. I know it is hard to think about, but on that day there are going to be people who have claimed Jesus as their own for years, and yet Jesus is not going to claim them … and for some, lack of active compassion will be the reason.

At this point you might be tempted to assume that I am painting the mission and purpose of God in our lives with a broad stroke of social justice. That is not what I am doing. However, there is no denying that in Matthew 25, two of the determining factors that will be used to separate the sheep from the goats are active love and real compassion.

I know how shocking this sounds. And uncomfortable. I suppose the idea is so uncomfortable because it is so far outside the box of how we approach God and the Christian faith. Though no one would necessarily put it in these words, many tend to approach faith as if one day God is going to ask us to present to Him a list of all the things we did not do during this life. So maybe your list would say, "I did not smoke, drink, have sex before marriage, or wear shorts to church." Someone else's list might say, "I did not curse, gamble, or get divorced." The list could unfold in a million different ways, but I think the predominant mind-set is that when we become Christians, we are to start avoiding certain behaviors known as sin, and in doing so we will become prepared for judgment day. If that is the approach you take toward God and faith, one day you will likely have an impressive list of behavior modifications to present to Jesus … and yet you just might find yourself surrounded by other goats.

You may get to heaven with your church clothes pressed and clean, expecting Jesus to say those beloved words, "Well done, My good and faithful servant"—and instead you may hear Him say, "Away from Me. I have no idea who you are." You might say, "Lord, Lord, don't You know about all of the behaviors I avoided because of my faith in You?" And again He will say, "I have no idea who you are."

If most of us were honest, I think we would have to admit that Matthew 25 paints a vastly different picture from what we tend to envision about judgment day. I am not sure what that day will be like, but there is no doubt going to be a lot of shock, sorrow, and disappointment. Some people will probably want to say, "Yeah, but—what about—well, how come …" but I don't think they will be given the opportunity to do so. Sadly, some great church people will be thrown into hell.

If Matthew 25 paints a picture of the end, many of us very likely need to experience a paradigm shift about the God and faith of the Bible.

FROM THOU SHALL NOT TO THOU SHALL

I do not believe for a second that I am supposed to earn my way to heaven, and I believe God's grace is more far-reaching than I could ever dream … but I believe that if Jesus had returned twelve years ago, I would have spent eternity in hell. That is a sobering statement, isn't it?

Here's the thing: if Jesus had returned twelve years ago, I would have been eager to meet Him. By that point in my life I had compiled a pretty incredible spiritual résumé. I had been going to church Sunday mornings, Sunday nights, and Wednesday nights my entire life; I could have counted on one hand how many times I had missed. I had already preached my first sermon. I had one year of Bible college education.

I had also compiled an impressive résumé of things I had *not* done. I had never tasted a drop of alcohol. I had never been to a dance (I was not allowed to dance because I was told it led to other things, which I have since learned it does: public humiliation). I had watched only one or two rated-R movies, had closed one eye during the bad parts, and had not made a habit of cussing. If Jesus had come back when I was nineteen years old, I would have marched right up to Him with my chin up and my chest puffed out, proud of the documentation I could give Him. I was more than prepared for Jesus to come back.

Or so I thought.

But I honestly believe that if Jesus had come back when I was nineteen, He would have looked at me and said, "I have no idea who you are. Away from Me." Given the opportunity, I would have protested "But, Jesus, don't You see all the things I have avoided doing in my life? Don't You see what my church attendance was like? Don't You see that I have even scolded people who haven't lived according to the Thou Shall Not list?" I don't think Jesus's mind would have changed.

The truth is, I spent the first nineteen years of my life believing in a Thou Shall Not God and living out my faith accordingly. Though I am far from being the perfect Christian, by the grace of God I have come to view and understand Him as a Thou Shall God. My great desire is to bring glory to God, and to do so I know that my heart needs to celebrate when His does and to break about the same things that break His.

Understanding God as a Thou Shall God does not in any way diminish the significance of obedience or morality—in fact, I would say quite the contrary is true. However, when you understand God as a Thou Shall God, you view obedience and morality as ways to honor God and spread His glory instead of as ways to impress Him.

Spreading the glory of God, then, is not so much about "what" but "who." In other words, to bring God the most glory in and through our lives we must reach out to, invest in, and care for people. And Jesus teaches in Matthew 25 that when we spend our lives doing these things, we are actually reaching out to, investing in, and caring for Him.

I don't know about you, but when I look through the lens of Matthew 25 at my everyday life, the opportunities abound. Suddenly I am no longer surrounded by a city full of faceless, nameless people. Instead, metaphorically speaking, I am surrounded by Jesus. Certainly we are called to reach out, invest in, and care for people, but to get practical, we need to get specific about the people who are close to the heart of God.

Though it is far too mechanical to label or categorize people, at least attempting to do so is helpful in identifying specific ways we can allow God to work through us in the lives of others. Certainly

God is honored anytime we invest our lives in other people for His glory, but as you study the Bible, you'll find three groups of people who are mentioned over and over again.

THE POOR

When we use Matthew 25 as the template, we see that as Jesus followers, we are called to be involved in the lives of the poor. Sure, the word *poor* is not mentioned in Matthew 25, but the inference can easily be made. People who are hungry, thirsty, and without clothing are almost always poor. *Poor* is a concept that certainly applies beyond the material realm, but Matthew 25 undoubtedly includes the concept of physical poverty.

I think most people would agree that the issue of poverty and how to effectively deal with it is quite complex. Some believe that poverty relief is the responsibility of the government—and the government certainly is playing a role through Food Stamps, WIC, and other similar programs. But the question is not whether the government is effectively relieving poverty but whether it is truly their obligation to do so.

Are you playing a role in relieving poverty? One day you will be held accountable for what you are or are not doing to address the issue. So will I. And while I would not suggest that the primary purpose of your life should be poverty relief, Jesus seems to teach that poverty should be an issue you take personally along the journey of your life.

As Jesus followers, we are at times shockingly good at rationalizing away our responsibilities. For instance, we can become consumed with determining why people are stuck in poverty. There is certainly a time and a place to study social and cultural issues in order to find long-term solutions for issues like homelessness. And undoubtedly some ways of helping people are far more effective than others, but a desire for bigger-picture problem solving should never serve as an excuse for not helping the poor.

I think many Christians have an incredible ability to create rational reasons not to help people. Perhaps not consciously, but definitely subconsciously. I literally have lost count of how many people have warned me not to give money to someone on the side of the street because "there is no way to know how they are going to use the money." Those warnings are often followed by very specific scenarios like, "You know they are spending the money on drugs, right?" or, "You know that money is going to enable their addiction to alcohol, right?" Of course there is a need for discernment when you make an intentional investment in another person's life—financial or otherwise—but all too often we allow such "wisdom" to serve as an excuse to do nothing.

Can you imagine how different Jesus's earthly life and ministry would have been if He had applied this supposed logic to His life? Most of the people Jesus served or invested in would have been left broken, alone, and marginalized because He could have easily rationalized that doing nothing was the best choice.

I suppose this is my struggle: How long can we as Christians continue to sit in restaurants enjoying a warm meal while we debate whether the person on the corner would have used money for drugs or for food? I am aware that there are many, many Christians who are actively involved in serving the poor and feeding the hungry—and I am so thankful for such efforts—but I also know there are too many people wearing the name of Christ who are completely content to do nothing for the poor.

If we look at Matthew 25 and shape our lives accordingly, doing nothing for the poor is not an option. There are so many ways the needy in your community can be served. No matter where you live, you probably have access to a career center where you can offer professional mentoring; food kitchens where you can cook and serve soup; clothing centers where you can donate or organize clothing—and the list goes on. All of these opportunities are available and legitimate, but let me get a little closer to the heart and mind of Jesus: invite a poor person or family to live in your home.

I know, I know. It sounds so irresponsible to bring a stranger into your home. What if they steal your stuff? What if they have a criminal record? What if they don't follow your "house rules"? I have asked these kinds of questions too and have allowed fear of the answers to keep me from intentionally welcoming someone in poverty to live in my home. Certainly there are legitimate questions and concerns to entertain before you invite someone to stay in your home, but don't allow your questions and concerns to keep you from doing something. Again, Matthew 25 doesn't allow "doing nothing" as an option for how to respond to the poor.

Last fall our church received word that a very run-down apartment complex in our community had been condemned. Honestly, the apartments probably needed to be condemned for safety and health reasons, but the problem was that the residents were given only about one week's notice. I remember walking down the church hallway to my office and noticing Erica, a young woman from our staff, putting on her coat, about to rush out the door. I stopped and asked, "Where are you going in such a hurry?" As I followed her to the door, she explained she was on her way to the condemned apartment complex.

"What are you going to do when you get there?" I asked.

She said, "I don't know, but that is where I need to be."

Over the next several days, Erica organized and executed an incredible plan to assist the residents in identifying new places to live and securing down payments for the new places. One afternoon that week I drove to the apartment complex to see what Erica had been up to, and I was blown away. She took me on a tour of the neighborhood, and I noticed immediately that not only did all the residents know her by name, but she knew all of them by name. She stopped and played with their children, offered hugs, and shared her cell phone with those who needed to make calls. When we walked into the office where she had set up makeshift headquarters, she nonchalantly offered me a spray can of bedbug repellant. As I drove toward my safe, warm, noninfested home that afternoon, I couldn't help but think that I had just spent time with Jesus. Erica is a young blonde woman, but for those few hours she looked an awful lot like Jesus to me. And even more so, as I met the residents and tried to make eye contact with them, I felt like I was making eye contact with Jesus.

Throughout the Bible is a clear call to be involved with the poor of this world. This might mean you work at a soup kitchen one night a week, but it also might mean that when the evening news tells a story about a condemned apartment complex, you rush out of the house instead of just turning the channel. When it comes to the poor of our communities, we cannot do everything, but we also cannot settle for doing nothing, especially if we are serious about the mission and purpose God has for our lives. You want to be holy? You may need a can of bedbug spray.

THE MARGINALIZED

There are many different types of people who likely feel marginalized in any community, but I don't know any people who are marginalized more than those in prison. They are sentenced to live hidden behind walls. Warning signs are posted on roads around the prison simply to alert any passersby to their existence. Prisoners live and oftentimes die in a cage. Let me be clear: I believe the Bible teaches there are and should be consequences for the decisions we make in regard to laws. In Romans 13 Paul teaches that the government is responsible to develop the law of the land and that the law should be obeyed. Therefore, prison can be an appropriate form of punishment—but nonetheless, the people who are placed behind bars are still people.

Marginalized people.

During Bible college I spent a significant amount of time in prison.

I suppose I need to clarify. I was not incarcerated, but I spent many days behind the walls of the Missouri State Penitentiary as part of a weekend prison-ministry group. Once a month for two years, I traveled several hours to the state penitentiary. When the group I went with arrived, the warden would escort us behind the walls into the protective custody unit, which might as well have been another planet. Many of the men I grew to know and love in that place were murderers, rapists, and molesters … but they were also followers of Jesus.

Jesus is alive and well behind the bars of prisons. At first I was shocked at the bright and bold faith exhibited by so many living in those circumstances, and yet the more I have come to know Jesus, the less shocked I have become. Of course there will be many behind bars who possess an undying faith in Jesus—they are near and dear to His heart, for they are the marginalized.

Now, I am not suggesting that Jesus values or invests more in people who are living outside the margins of any society than those inside those same margins. However, as you study Jesus's life and ministry, you can't deny that He had a unique passion for those living outside the margins.

I could turn to many examples, but perhaps none better captures Jesus's disposition toward and passion for the marginalized people of society than the story we already looked at in John 4.

In the passage we find Jesus's encounter with the woman at the well. Yeah, that woman. The one who had been married five times and was living with yet another man. I want to be careful and not fill in too many blanks about her life, but there is no presumption in identifying her as a woman living outside the margins of society. We have already unpacked Jesus's encounter with the woman, but we realize His passion for the marginalized people of society, especially this woman, when we find out from the text that this meeting was not by accident but by design. Jesus's meeting with the woman at the well was not a diversion from His schedule; this meeting was His schedule.

As chapter 4 begins, we read, "Now [Jesus] had to go through Samaria." The words to note in that sentence are *had to*. If you don't understand those words, you cannot understand this passage. There was a well-traveled path that went around Samaria. That path was well traveled for a reason: no Jew worth his salt would have willingly traveled into Samaria, especially when there was a clear-cut alternative. So geographically speaking, Jesus didn't have to go through Samaria … yet He *had to* go through Samaria. His GPS could have taken Him a different way, but His heart demanded that He go through Samaria. Bottom line: Jesus didn't accidentally run into this broken, lonely, marginalized Samaritan woman at the well. He intentionally chose an itinerary that led Him right to her.

Our call to invest in and care for the marginalized of our society is not a "when and if you get around to it and happen to run into someone who is marginalized," but a "you set your schedule intentionally to involve people living outside the margins of society."

What I find so fascinating is that when we invest in and care for marginalized people, not only are we loving like Jesus loves, but we are loving Jesus. He said, "I was in prison and you came to visit me" (Matt. 25:36). Perhaps the reason we so often miss Jesus is because we look for a person wearing a white robe and blue sash instead of a person wearing a bright orange jumpsuit with a number on the front or a woman with a scarlet letter around her neck and a water basin in her hands.

THE SICK

The shortest verse in the Bible simply says, "Jesus wept" (John 11:35). Perhaps you envision a single large tear creeping down Jesus's cheek before He quickly wipes it away. And yes, the Greek word for *wept* denotes a private, quiet mourning. However, in an earlier verse we are told that Jesus was "deeply troubled" (v. 33 NLT). This phrase, *deeply troubled*, in the Greek communicates a loud, public grief. So perhaps for a moment He wiped a single tear from His cheek, but before and after doing so He just may have been doubled over, drowning in a pool of His own tears. This is Jesus crying until the tears are no more. When the Bible says Jesus was deeply troubled, He was deeply troubled. He cried. He wailed. He wept.

Why?

You might know this verse is tucked away in the story about Lazarus's death. Lazarus's sisters, Mary and Martha, had sent a messenger four days earlier to let Jesus know that Lazarus was very sick—that he was knocking on death's door. One would assume Jesus would have immediately hit the pause button on His itinerant ministry and sprinted to Lazarus's bedside to do something. Instead, He literally did nothing. In fact, by the time He showed up to the small town of Bethany where Lazarus lived, Lazarus had already been dead four days. Understandably, Mary and Martha chastised Jesus for not showing up sooner. After all, if He was able to command the wind and the waves to die down, then surely He could have told the sickness to subside—but He didn't, and so it didn't.

And yet Jesus wept. Jesus wept at the death of Lazarus, but it isn't difficult to envision that even when Jesus first learned of Lazarus's sickness, He was deeply troubled as well. Why would He have wept before death arrived? I would assert that it's because sickness leads to death, and Jesus's heart breaks for those dealing with sickness and death, because sickness and death were never a part of His original plan. And so every time sickness of any shape, size, or seriousness sets in, it is another brutal reminder that sin and death have hijacked this world. His world.

God promises that the day is coming when all things will be made right, but in the meantime, while everything is so wrong, He is committed to being near the weary and brokenhearted.

Jesus stays near, and so should we as His followers—

to the bedside,

the cancer ward,

the dialysis unit,

the Alzheimer's wing,

the children's hospital,

the mental institution.

If Jesus were walking the face of planet earth today, undoubtedly we would at times find Him preaching to stadiums full of people, but more often we would find Him kneeling beside a sick person, tears streaming down His face. If we wanted to find Jesus, we would be more likely to do so at the closest hospice facility than at the closest church facility.

• • •

Whether in regard to the poor, the marginalized, or the sick, compassion is not an emotion but a motion. As Jesus's followers, we cannot settle for a generic brand of compassion that simply moves our hearts; we must have a compassion that moves our muscles.

• • •

Almost a decade ago I moved to Louisville, Kentucky, to begin a one-year preaching internship. A month or so after moving to this new city, I met a man who would become one of my best friends. The first time I saw him, he was standing on the corner of the exit ramp near where I lived. He was hard to miss. Very tall and lanky, with a long scraggly beard, he had a cigarette in one hand and a cardboard sign in the other. I cannot remember what his sign said, but I know it included the word *hungry*. I pulled into a nearby parking lot and walked across the busy exit ramp to speak with him. I explained that I wanted to provide a meal for him, and we both agreed that the best place to go was the McDonald's across the street. I figured that going across the street would be quick and easy, but that was before I realized he was physically handicapped. I am still not sure exactly what was wrong, but one of his feet did not function properly, and so he essentially had to drag that leg. Nearly half an hour later, we finally arrived at McDonald's. Embarrassed about his appearance, Mike did not want to go inside the restaurant, so I ordered the food and met him outside. That meal began a relationship that lasted for the next eighteen months. Numerous times a week I would search for him. Sometimes we would share a meal; other times we would simply share conversation. Building a relationship with Mike gave me my first opportunity to get an up-close glimpse of severe poverty. Mike was in his early thirties but appeared to be in his midfifties. The lines on his face hinted at his story and the pain, suffering, and rejection he had endured during his young life. Mike often talked about some distant relatives in West Virginia, but he seemed resigned to the fact that he would never be with them again. I knew him well, but I never was able to fully determine how or why he ended up spending his days on the street. All I know is that he did. He spent his nights in a place a bit more comfortable, but only a bit.

One night he asked if I could give him a ride to his place. I assumed we were heading to an apartment somewhere. Finally he gestured for me to turn into a dark parking lot. For a moment I thought perhaps I had made myself too vulnerable, but the dark parking lot was where his temporary place of residence sat parked. Apparently a local bar owner had given him permission to sleep inside an old, broken-down conversion van in the back of the parking lot. In the time that I knew him, Mike spent most of his nights inside that van. A few times he stayed with me to eat pizza, watch wrestling, and do laundry, but usually the van was his home.

I still occasionally think about Mike, and every time I visit Louisville, I hope that I will find him again. I have also often wondered if the help I was able to provide during that year and a half made any lasting difference in his life. I do know one thing for sure: for eighteen months I spent many dark nights—sitting behind a gas station or standing outside a broken-down conversion van—with Jesus.

Ironic, isn't it? I spent a year of my life working at one of the largest churches in North America, and yet the times I found myself closest to Jesus were when I was standing outside a conversion van or behind a trash receptacle in a gas-station parking lot. This is another example of what many have coined the "upside-down way of Jesus." Jesus taught that if you want to live, you first have to die. If you want to be first, you have to be last. If you want to be great, you need to become the least. And if you want to sense His presence, don't hang out in church buildings but in places like dark alleys, gas-station parking lots, and soup kitchens. Jesus didn't really say the last line, but He might as well have done so.

Now, I am hesitant to share stories such as these because you may get the impression that I am looking to be the hero of the story. However, nothing could be further from the truth. For every night I have spent in a parking lot with someone who was down and out, there have been a hundred opportunities I have failed to seize. For every time I have spoken up on behalf of the poor, the weak, and the marginalized of this world, there are so many other times I have stayed as quiet as a church mouse. Times when instead of standing up for them or moving any muscle on their behalf I have relaxed in my recliner and spent the night in front of the TV.

What about you?

REFLECT & DISCUSS

1. According to Jesus, active compassion will serve as a determining factor in whether you are labeled as a sheep or a goat on judgment day. What emotions does that idea stir up inside of you? Fear? Anxiety? Anticipation? Relief?
2. Most people are quick to label themselves as being compassionate. If you do claim to be compassionate, is it because of emotion? Or motion?
3. There is no way to meet every need. However, think about practical ways you could meet some needs in your community in the name of Jesus.

4. Jesus said, "Whatever you did for one of the least of these … you did for me" (Matt. 25:40). Does reflecting on those words of Jesus change the way you perceive the poor, sick, and marginalized? If so, how?

5. Intentionally choose an active compassion opportunity. Seize it. Then reflect upon what God accomplished in you and through you because of your active compassion.

PRAYER

Father, there are so many people with so many needs. Clearly, I am unable to do everything, but do not let me feel comfortable in doing nothing. Move my heart, but also move my muscles into action. When a decision has to be made, help me to err on the side of activity instead of passivity, generosity instead of caution. When I look into the eyes of those in need, teach me to see You and then to respond accordingly. Forgive me for the times I have been content to sit and do nothing, all while claiming to be compassionate. Thank You for living out active compassion by coming from heaven to earth to meet a need I never could have: my own need for grace and forgiveness. In Jesus's name.

Chapter 5

ADVOCATE

I do not like the word *religion*.

In so many ways, this word and idea has been twisted and tainted and brings along a lot of associated baggage. Therefore, though I unapologetically claim to be a follower of Jesus, I often deny being religious. The problem is not the idea of religion; the problem is with what religion has become. Religion often turns into going through certain motions, completing lists of responsibilities, celebrating traditions, and checking off boxes on a list of to-dos and not-to-dos.

Religion can be noble, right, and good, but no amount of religious activity is worthwhile if done in place of experiencing intimacy with God.

The idea of religion needs to be redeemed. When we read the New Testament book of James, we can see that religion seemingly had lost a lot of meaning in the days of the early church as well. As much as things change, some things always stay the same. Perhaps only a few years after Jesus had returned to heaven, religious duty had already replaced living for Jesus. For some reason or another, James felt compelled to redefine the type of religion God finds acceptable. By the way—defining a religion God finds acceptable defines at the same time religion God does not find acceptable.

James wrote, "Religion that God our Father accepts as pure and faultless is this: to look after orphans and widows in their distress" (James 1:27).

Religion that God the Father accepts as pure and faultless is not complicated; in fact, this religion is quite simplistic. The truth is, many people would read this definition of religion and feel like a lot has been left out. And we have to be oh so careful not to line the Scriptures up with the way we are already living, but to line up our lives with the Scriptures.

If we allow the faith we are living to define what we believe is religion that God finds acceptable and pure, then the blanks would quite likely be filled in this way:

Religion God our Father accepts as pure and faultless is … meeting in the church building as often as possible.

Religion God our Father accepts as pure and faultless is … being involved in multiple Bible studies.

Religion God our Father accepts as pure and faultless is … filling up our life calendar with as many church activities as possible.

But James defines religion in a different way.

To be fair, James does add another line to his definition of godly religion: "And to keep oneself from being polluted by the world." This is where sin avoidance indeed plays a role in living a life that brings glory to God. The seriousness of sin cannot be excluded from this or any conversation involving bringing glory to God. In our culture of acceptance, it can be tempting to focus on social justice aspects of the gospel at the expense of speaking openly and lovingly about the reality and danger of sin. In fact, in many Christian circles the word *sin* is not even used anymore. But it is important to use Bible terms for Bible ideas.

Keeping oneself from being polluted by the world is front and center in any discussion about religion God accepts as pure and faultless. I think the very reason a book like this one is necessary is because there is a tendency to focus on one aspect of godly religion or the other. Some people place a great premium on issues of social justice while ignoring the call to stay pure in this world. On the other hand, some focus so much on not being influenced by the world that they don't take seriously the call to social justice, especially in terms of caring for orphans and widows.

Regardless of which side of the continuum you may be consumed with, just fulfilling one aspect of godly religion is not what pleases God. When people spend their entire lives investing in social justice issues but blend into the world all too well, God is not honored. And He isn't honored by people who have a mile-long list of ways they have avoided being polluted by the world but have never donated a dollar or spent an afternoon or opened up a room in their house to care for an orphan or widow in distress.

So, using James 1:27 as a template, how are you doing in terms of living a life of religion that God would find pure and faultless? I know answering this question and others like it can be uncomfortable, but they are necessary if we are serious about honoring God and spreading His glory.

Here are a few more questions you may want to ask yourself to help evaluate how you are doing in terms of godly religion:

Can you name more than one widow or widower?

Have you had this person into your home to share a meal or a holiday?

What, if anything, are you doing to advocate for an orphaned or vulnerable child?

Do you pray for the foster children in your community?

Have you asked God if one of the foster children in your community needs to call you Mom or Dad?

In our twenty-first-century American Christian culture, just like with caring for the poor, it is all too easy to forsake the call to advocate for orphans and widows in distress because there are so many governmental support systems in place that often provide such care and attention. Certainly there is a role the government can play, but their role should be secondary at best compared to the role Jesus followers play in the care of such people.

Take a look around your community, and undoubtedly you will find that many of the nursing homes, convalescent centers, and children's homes are named after or funded by the church in some way, and that is admirable. However, that reality does not diminish the responsibility each individual Christian has to care for, invest in, and advocate for widows and orphans.

ORPHANS

I am fortunate to serve as pastor of a congregation where many have taken seriously the call to care for orphans, especially in terms of adoption. There are many in our congregation who were abandoned as young children but now know what it is to be chosen.

Adoption is near to the heart of God. In fact, He is an adoptive Father in the truest sense of the word. All throughout the Bible, adoption is the language used to talk about our relationship to God. Yes, as Christians we are God's children, but we are adopted children. Despite the fact that all Christians are God's adopted children, there are still some common misconceptions about adoption in our culture. Sometimes the term *adopted child* can cause people to think a child is somehow lesser. Quite to the contrary—being an adopted child is perhaps even more significant than simply being a biological child. The reason is quite simple: every single adopted child has been chosen. A child never accidentally becomes adopted. An adoption is a long, thorough, intentional, and oftentimes very expensive process. From God's perspective, His adoption process was long, thorough, intentional, and very expensive. For God to adopt us as His children required more than a complicated dossier and a large check. God paid the highest price: He sent His son to die.

Why is God so passionate about the plight of orphans? I assert that it is because the adoption process is one of the clearest reflections of His own love. When we care for orphans, we are meeting not merely a sociological need but a theological need. We provide a family while at the same time putting a God-type love on display for all to see and for some to experience.

The longer I have served as a pastor, the more I have seen this reality in regard to adoption: some people are experts at creating excuses of why adoption would never be possible for them, while other families are experts at eliminating any obstacles that would hinder them from adopting. When it comes to eliminating obstacles, two families in particular come to my mind; both attend the church

I serve. At last count, one family has nine children, six of whom are adopted. The other family currently has five children, three of whom are adopted. And the sixth is on his way from Africa.

Sometimes—and I have been guilty of this myself—people respond to these stories by coming up with reasons why those families are capable of orphan care so they can justify in their minds why they personally are not. *Yeah, but they have a lot of money.* Or, *Yeah, but they have a big house.* Or, *Yeah, but they have a nice family minibus.* These statements may or may not be true, but what is true is that instead of finding a way to emulate this incredible example, people come up with a list of reasons why personally doing so would be impossible.

In no way am I suggesting that every Christian family is called to adopt. What I am saying is that many of us are equipped to do more for orphans than we allow ourselves to imagine. Would doing so require a lifestyle alteration or two? Probably. Would doing so be expensive? Possibly. Would doing so at times seem inconvenient? Likely. But would doing so be worth it? Depends on who you ask.

But 153 million orphans worldwide say yes.

God says yes.

After all, spiritually, He is an adoptive Father hundreds of millions of times over.

Beyond adopting, there are so many other practical ways to invest in the orphans of this world:

- Sponsor a child through a child-relief organization.
- Serve as a foster family for children in your community.

- Volunteer at a local children's home.
- Financially invest in a family who has chosen adoption.

Whatever it looks like, be sure that orphan care is weaved into the very fabric of your life and faith. Intentionally loving orphans is the clearest reflection of God's love for us.

WIDOWS

In our congregation we have a policy that no widow or widower stands alone—but that policy was instituted in the Christian community long before our congregation existed. In the book of Acts, as the church was just getting started, already there was an emphasis placed on caring for the practical needs of the widows within the body of Christ. In fact, in Acts 6 the first deacons were appointed for the very purpose of caring for the needs of the widows. Widows and widowers are inevitably going to experience loneliness because of their great loss, but never should they be left alone to try to make sense of the financial implications of losing their spouse, to manage a home, or to deal with the tedious task of making funeral preparations.

Hopefully there is a noticeable trend here. Never should widows or widowers be left to stand alone in their life or in their faith. Some have suggested single parents may be the new widows in the life of the church, and I agree. The single parents in your circle of influence may not necessarily be dealing with the grief of death, but they are likely dealing with equally difficult emotions such as abandonment, insecurity, and fear. The feelings associated with divorce are often compared to the feelings associated with death. In an effort to stand next to the widows and widowers, do not overlook or ignore the single parents among you. Their official status may not be the same, but their burden is real and heavy—too much to be carried while standing alone.

Whatever season of life you find yourself in, make every imaginable effort to ensure that woven into the very fabric of your life is an emphasis on caring for and advocating for widows and widowers and single parents in your circle of influence and beyond. Perhaps such an emphasis will mean you make a weekly visit to a nursing home. Perhaps you will become quite familiar with doctors' offices and pharmacies. Perhaps you will often find yourself pulling up an extra chair to the dinner table, mowing an extra lawn, making another bed, giving an extra bath, or offering free child care so a parent can work. Whatever the implications may be in your life as a follower of Jesus, do not stop anywhere short of advocating for widows and widowers in their distress. Perhaps the widows and widowers you are associated with do not seem to be in distress, and so you feel excused from the responsibility. You can be sure that regardless of what the external appearance may suggest, someone who has experienced the loss of his or her spouse is living with a level of distress. We cannot completely eliminate the feelings of distress, but as Christians we are called to ease the distress.

The work of advocating for widows and orphans will not always feel glamorous, but the effort and investment will always be applauded. Perhaps not by the one you are helping, but certainly by the One who created the one you are helping.

REFLECT & DISCUSS

1. If religion God accepts is about caring for widows and orphans in their distress, how are you doing? What, if any, changes need to be made to your life and faith?

2. Name the widows and widowers you know on a personal basis. Think about practical ways to regularly invest in their lives.

3. Spend time praying and reflecting about how you can advocate for orphans. Do you sense God nudging you to sponsor a child? Provide foster care? Adopt a child or children? If you sense God nudging you, do not ignore Him; instead put a plan in place to carry out His desires for you.

PRAYER

Father, You are an advocate for widows and orphans; teach me to be the same on Your behalf. Provide the opportunities, resources, and vision to ensure that all widows, widowers, single parents, orphans, and vulnerable children are being loved. Adoption is a beautiful picture of Your love for me. I pray You would remove obstacles that are currently hindering adoption efforts both domestically and internationally. In terms of adoption, allow those who are willing and ready to carry out Your will on earth as it is in heaven to do so. In Jesus's name.

Chapter 6

SERVE

What would Jesus look like if He were in ministry today?

Of course, Jesus is in ministry in and through His church and by the power of the Holy Spirit, but I mean in a more tangible way: What would Jesus's ministry look like if He were on the earth right now? If we could visit the church where He shaped the culture, what would we find? If we could interview Him about preferences in regard to worship and dress and ministry strategy, what would He say?

You may have wondered this as well, because it sure would be nice to know Jesus is on our side when we draw our battle lines over such important issues, right? Would Jesus be a contemporary worship guy, or would He lean in the direction of traditional? Would He be a suit-and-tie guy or a jeans-and-untucked-shirt guy? Would He establish an attractional or missional culture within the local church? And what about technology? Would He prefer PC or Mac? (Okay, I think we all know the answer to that one. After all, God was the original inventor of the Apple.)

Asking these questions is a bit of an exercise in futility. We can take some guesses about what Jesus would look like if He were in ministry today, but we really can't say for sure. The twenty-first-century American church is in a very different time and place than first-century Jewish culture, so undoubtedly Jesus would have a bit of a different appearance now than He did then. So if Jesus walked through the doors of your church building or mine, I am pretty confident He would not be wearing a white robe and baby-blue sash, but beyond that I really don't know.

But here is one thing I do know: whether Jesus would wear jeans or a suit and tie, whether He'd sport a pair of black-rimmed glasses, whether He'd be carrying a backpack or a briefcase, whether He'd be clean shaven or have a bit of stubble on His face, whether He'd prefer tapping His toes to the Gaithers or humming a Chris Tomlin tune … in His hands He would be carrying a basin and a towel. As much as things change, some things always stay the same.

You might know the story. John 13, the final night of Jesus's life.

> It was just before the Passover Festival. Jesus knew that the hour had come for him to leave this world and go to the Father. Having loved his own who were in the world, he loved them to the end.
>
> The evening meal was in progress, and the devil had already prompted Judas, the son of Simon Iscariot, to betray Jesus. Jesus knew that the Father had put all things under his power, and that he had come from God and was returning to God; so he got up from the meal, took off his outer clothing,

and wrapped a towel around his waist. After that,
he poured water into a basin and began to wash his
disciples' feet, drying them with the towel that was
wrapped around him. (John 13:1–5)

More than anyone else Jesus deserved to have His feet washed.
Not only were His feet caked with red clay from the Palestinian roads,
but also in just a few hours His feet would be caked with red blood
as they dangled from the cross. However in that small upper room
instead of being washed, Jesus did the washing. Sometimes when this
text is discussed, there is a sense of astonishment about what took
place—shock that Jesus lowered Himself to the task reserved for the
lowest servant in the household. I find the idea of the Creator washing the feet of His creation captivating but not necessarily shocking.
We are told that before Jesus began washing feet, He took off His
outer garment. *For Jesus, the basin and the towel were not just a good
sermon prop; they were the song of His life.* I wish I could tell you the
same has always been true about my life.

I attended a small Christian college in the Midwest. The summer
after my third sophomore year (I wish I were kidding about that
part), I served on a camp team. Camp teams are usually made up of
four people—two girls and two guys—and for an entire summer, the
team travels from one junior/senior high church camp to another.
As you might imagine, I have a lot of interesting memories from
that summer, but I most distinctly remember the last night of our
last week of camp. It was Thursday night, a night full of weeping
and gnashing of teeth. Actually just weeping as many girls in camp
went to the front of the stage at invitation time genuinely desiring to

commit their lives to Christ. And every junior high boy would come up front at invitation time too, not because any of them wanted to rededicate their lives, but because there were crying girls to hug. Well, I had been asked to preach that night. I didn't have a whole lot of material with me to work from, but I do remember I decided to preach on a lifestyle of selfless service. As a team we came up with a creative element that would help teach the concept. We invited thirteen camp leaders to come up in front of the stage, and while I preached the John 13 passage, the other three members of my team used a basin and a towel to wash their feet.

The next morning camp ended, and we packed up the van and drove home. Several weeks later I had a meeting with the leader of the camp teams. The purpose of the meeting was to sift through the evaluations from the various camp directors in regard to how we had done as a camp team both corporately and individually. I will never forget when my evaluation was read from that last week of camp. As the evaluation began, the camp director mentioned what a powerful sermon I had preached, and my chest began to swell up with pride … but it didn't last long. Next, the leader read, "Jamie preached a great sermon on selfless service, but he didn't live it out that week." At the time I was incredibly defensive and even held a personal grudge against the camp director for a while, but he was right. It is one thing to *talk about* a basin-and-towel life; it is another thing to *live* a basin-and-towel life.

In Matthew 28:19 Jesus said, "Go and make disciples of all nations." If you take the liberty to combine those words with Jesus's other teachings and His lifestyle, it isn't hard to hear Him saying, "Go with a basin and a towel, and make disciples of all nations." He may not have said those exact words with His lips, but He shouted them with His life.

We all face a common hindrance that in many cases keeps us from living a life of selfless service. If you want to see it, you need to look no further than a mirror: our greatest hindrance is self. Living in a self-centered culture makes it hard to cultivate and maintain a lifestyle of selflessness. In such a technology-driven society, self-promotion is easier than ever. In a matter of minutes, you can have your own Twitter feed, Facebook account, YouTube channel, and blog space. I am not suggesting that we should not use the technology that's available to us, because it can absolutely serve a godly purpose. But easily—so easily—we can slide into a life of self-promotion without even recognizing it is happening. Here is the distinct difference between self-promotion and selfless service: through self-promotion we become famous; through selfless service Jesus becomes famous.

I suppose someone who didn't know any better would assume that Christians wouldn't struggle with or settle for a life of self-promotion. One would think that the people who appear to be the closest to Jesus would struggle the *least* with self-promotion, but in many cases these people struggle the *most* with self-promotion.

Go back to the upper room in John 13 for a moment. I could wax eloquent about possible reasons one of the disciples didn't pick up the basin and the towel. Some may argue God had set the stage so Jesus could teach this divine lesson. And it is possible that each of the disciples just assumed, *Someone else will do it*. A lot of selfless service goes undone based upon the "someone else will do it" assumption.

Someone else will work on the parking team.

Someone else will prepare the Communion.

Someone else will mow the lawn.

Someone else will clean the bathrooms.

Someone else will wash the feet.

It could be that the disciples were looking around the room, assuming someone else would do it, but I don't think that is what happened. The more likely answer? The disciples didn't get down to wash feet because they were engaged in yet another discussion about which one of them was the greatest. It wasn't the first time. The Gospels tell us that on at least three other occasions the conversation took place about which of them was greatest in the kingdom of heaven. They wrestled with questions like these:

Who would sit on Jesus's right hand and left hand
  when He assumed the throne?
Who would get the corner office?
Who would be given the most prestigious position?

My guess is that these weren't necessarily three separate conversations—more likely it was just an ongoing conversation that resumed any time they had the opportunity. So as they gathered around the table that night to share this meal with Jesus, it isn't at all hard to imagine they were back at it, debating which one really was the greatest. And so it was likely that in the midst of this conversation about who was the greatest one, the Greatest One got down on His hands and knees and washed feet.

In that small upper room in Jerusalem, the very people who appeared to be closest to Jesus got lost in self-promotion. As much as things change, some things always stay the same.

A couple of years ago I found myself sitting in a room in Orlando, Florida, with church leaders from all across the country. It was a Who's Who list of Christian leadership; these people were sought-after speakers, published authors, leaders of some of America's most well-known and influential churches ... and then there was me. (I don't know why I was invited, either.) At one point during the meeting, one of the men was asked why he had stopped writing a blog, or something to that effect. The man being questioned was a published author, so they just couldn't understand why he had stopped writing. He tried to skirt the question for a bit, but after being pressed he explained that he had stopped doing some of his public work because he had taken a vow of personal obscurity. He went on to explain that he didn't want to take the risk of chasing after self-promotion. His explanation sounded an awful lot like what John the Baptist once said: "He must become greater; I must become less" (John 3:30). Over the next few minutes, it was almost as if he was being chastised by the group for taking such a vow.

We were gathered in Florida, but for a few minutes we may as well have been gathered in a small upper room in Jerusalem. I am not saying that as Christians we have forsaken the call to pick up the basin and the towel; I am saying there is a great temptation to do so, to settle for self-promotion. And I understand why we feel so tempted to forsake the basin-and-towel lifestyle: it goes so against the grain of everything we have been taught by our culture. The way our culture measures value is that the higher you go, the more valuable you are. For example, in the Olympics the person who wins the gold medal does not stand on the bottom level of the podium; they stand on the top. In an organizational chart, the desired position is not the bottom; it is the top. High-powered corporate executives usually do not have offices on the first floor of the headquarters building; their office is oftentimes in the corner of the top floor. The penthouse condo is never on the first floor; it is always on the top floor. Success by the world's standards can be measured vertically: the more successful you are, the higher you go; the higher you go, the more valuable you are.

As we live and lead in such a culture, the basin-and-towel lifestyle doesn't come easy. If you live the basin-and-towel life, you will most likely never become famous—but Jesus will.

The lower you get, the less impressive you may seem, but the more like Jesus you look. You probably agree that the world doesn't need to see more of us; they need to see more of Jesus.

Several months ago we received an email at our church office about a young couple named Rick and Amy who were desperately in need. Rick was struggling to make ends meet, Amy was battling several forms of cancer that was thought to be terminal, they had three small children, and, oh yeah, they lived in a run-down trailer with no electricity.

Gary is an eighty-something-year-old former electrical engineer who used to lead our benevolence team at the church, so the information was given to him. Honestly—and I am not proud to admit this—in the midst of the hustle and bustle of leadership, I forgot all about the email, but Gary didn't. Because it was the Christmas season, Rick was able to secure a seasonal job at a local warehouse, but he didn't have any transportation. Gary picked him up every morning and drove him to work, and twelve hours later when Rick's shift was over, Gary was there waiting to drive him back home. Some generous person in our congregation donated a car, and Gary worked diligently to get insurance and tags for it and then gave it to Rick and Amy. Several weeks passed, and I didn't hear anything until I received an email late on a Monday night asking if I was available to do two baptisms. It was Rick and Amy.

As we were standing together backstage, I said, "I have heard bits and pieces of your story, but would you be willing to share it with me personally?" Before I even finished the question, Amy began sharing with me every detail of their lives and the struggles they had been dealing with for the last several years. She talked of the difficulty of raising three children while struggling financially, the recurring bouts with cancer, and the nauseating chemotherapy she had endured. She explained that the day before they received the donated car, she had been riding home on a city bus from her chemotherapy treatment and had to get off at a random bus stop because she was so sick from the treatment that she couldn't stop vomiting on the bus. As she was talking, one question kept stirring in my mind, and when she took a breath I finally asked, "In the midst of all the difficulty you have faced, in the face of so many agonizing circumstances, what has led you to make this decision to surrender your life to Jesus?" Without a moment's hesitation she said one of the most simple yet profound statements I have ever heard. It literally took my breath away. Amy said, "We realized that God is on our side."

It doesn't get any more theologically rich than that, right? In the midst of unemployment and hunger pangs and terminal cancer, they came to the conclusion that God was on their side. They didn't say this, but I cannot help but wonder if it had an awful lot to do with an eighty-something-year-old man named Gary who lives every day with a basin and a towel.

Somehow, it is when you take the posture of a servant that people catch a glimpse of the King.

I don't think anyone questions that foot washing is a selfless act. But here is where I think the problem arises: there is a tendency to think about selfless service as being just one possible lifestyle option. There are a variety of approaches toward the Christian life, and the basin-and-towel lifestyle is just one of the numerous options. You can see the problem, right? If selfless service is just one option of many, then it is rarely going to be chosen because when there are other options, who chooses the bottom rung on the ladder? Sure, there are a variety of ways to share the good news of Jesus with a lost and dying world, but selfless service is not just one of those ways. Selfless service should be the common denominator.

So take a meal to the new family on the street, but wash feet.

Take the evening shift with a baby so the new mother can get rest, but wash feet.

Teach Sunday school, but wash feet.

Build a Habitat for Humanity house, but wash feet.

Work in the nursery at church, but wash feet (and probably your hands, too).

Selfless service is not just *a* Christian lifestyle; it is *the* Christian lifestyle. Mark 10:45 says, "Even the Son of Man did not come to be served, but to serve."

In Jesus's day any time people entered a home, they needed to have their feet washed, and for good reason. The people back then traveled everywhere on the hot, dusty roads, so by the time they reached their destination, their feet were covered in red clay. Maybe people now do not have red mud caked on their feet, but there are dirty feet everywhere in your town, in your neighborhood, in your church, maybe even in your home. The question is not, "Are there dirty feet?" The question is, "Are you willing to wash the dirty feet that are all around you?"

WHAT IF?

So on a practical level, what does this all look like? I will be the first to tell you I don't have all the answers when it comes to selfless service, but I have found that some of the best service results from simply asking questions.

Several years ago I taught a series of messages entitled "Dangerous." The whole premise is that if you asked someone on the street in the first century to describe the church for you in one word, you just might hear the word *dangerous*. The first church was dangerous. Acts 17 tells us that they were accused of turning the world upside down for Christ. No doubt part of the reason the name of Jesus was literally spreading like wildfire is because the first church was a people of the basin and the towel. As I began the series I preached a message on sharing the scandalous grace of Jesus with our community. Whether we realize it or not, I believe all of us have lines drawn on how far God's grace goes, and so I wanted to challenge our people to intentionally stretch the boundaries of God's grace in our community. I didn't go to the stage with all of the answers; instead I went to the stage with one question: "What if?" Then I began filling in the blanks.

- What if we parked our church vans outside of local clubs on Saturday nights, waiting to be designated drivers?
- What if we took gifts to the office of the local abortion doctor just to let him know that he is made in the image of God and he is loved?
- What if some women in our congregation developed a ministry for the exotic dancers in our community so they could know that their value is not in how they look out of their clothes but in Christ and Christ alone?

I asked, "What if?" one more time, and then I walked off the stage. As I went to my seat, a young woman came up to me with tears streaming down her face and said, "When you mentioned the ministry to exotic dancers, I felt like you were talking right to me." I never dreamed someone would respond to the opportunity so quickly, and I certainly never dreamed my wife would be that someone.

Within just a few weeks my wife, Alex, along with a few other women from our church, had devised a plan about how they were going to take Jesus into the darkness of Emerald City. At the time, our church just happened to be doing a school-supply drive, so the women decided they would simply walk into the local club on a Friday afternoon and ask if there were any single mothers they could assist by offering school supplies. They did just that, and taking school supplies quickly turned into taking warm meals every Friday for lunch, which became taking meals every Friday evening as well for the next six months or so. Every Friday they would gather in the parking lot and pray that the light of Jesus would shine in the darkness of that place, and then they would take the meals into the dressing room and begin serving. While eating, the girls poured out their hearts about the brokenness of the lifestyle and how they felt so empty and worthless. After six months or so, the owner of the club met the women from our church at the door one night and informed them they were no longer welcome. Though I was disappointed, it didn't surprise me; Satan doesn't like it when Jesus shows up on his playground.

I wish I could tell you that during those six months at least fifteen exotic dancers began following Jesus. That would be a great ending to the story, but that is not what happened. I don't know how the story will end, but I do know that for six months, every Friday night Jesus was seen in a sleazy strip club in Florida because a small group of women decided to live the basin-and-towel life.

In Philippians 2:5–11 the apostle Paul wrote,

> In your relationships with one another, have the
> same mindset as Christ Jesus:
>
> Who, being in very nature God,
>   did not consider equality with God something
>   to be used to his own advantage;
> rather, he made himself nothing
>   by taking the very nature of a servant,
>   being made in human likeness.
> And being found in appearance as a man,
>   he humbled himself

by becoming obedient to death—
even death on a cross!

Therefore God exalted him to the highest place
and gave him the name that is above every
name,
that at the name of Jesus every knee should bow,
in heaven and on earth and under the earth,
and every tongue acknowledge that Jesus Christ is
Lord.

Do you serve? Or are you a servant? You may think I just asked the same question in two different ways, but I did not. I look at my own life, and I can readily and honestly claim that I seize many opportunities to serve, but I am more hesitant to claim that I live as a servant. There is a very significant distinction between serving and being a servant.

You see, serving is many times done on our terms. We identify opportunities that fit well within our gift set, or—if we are being really honest—we often choose service opportunities within our comfort zone. I do. I am quick to serve when I know the task is one I can easily and comfortably handle. For instance, a few months ago my wife organized an auction event for some underresourced individuals in our church. Numerous items had been donated to the church, and each person at the auction was given a certain amount of fake money they could use to bid on the items they wanted the most. I served on that particular night as the amateur auctioneer. Trust me, doing so was not a sacrifice on my behalf. I already talk very fast, I enjoy hearing myself talk, and I have secretly wondered what it would be like to be an auctioneer. Everyone had fun at the event, needs were met, and I got to talk until my voice was raspy and dry.

Though there was value in my willingness to serve on behalf of that ministry, doing so required very little of me. I did so on my terms, in a way that was comfortable for me. Sometimes serving falls within those very parameters, but oftentimes it does not.

The question every Christian must wrestle with at some point is this: Do you serve only when the opportunity is convenient and comfortable? Even then service is valuable to the one serving and the one being served; however, we are not merely called to serve but to be servants.

Service can be done on our own terms: when, where, how, and for whom we choose.

Not so with servants.

Servants serve anytime. Anywhere. Anyone.

Ironically, though Jesus came as a servant, He also came as Lord.

Lord. The word appears around 750 times in the New Testament. It is especially important to pay attention to how it's used in the Gospels as it relates to Jesus. Jesus is often called Lord in the Gospels. You'll also find that Jesus commonly referred to Himself as Lord. If you are not careful, you can completely miss out on what is being communicated when the word *Lord* is used in reference to Jesus. Perhaps even more likely is that you will miss out on what Jesus was communicating when He referred to Himself as Lord.

The natural idea we associate with the word *Lord* is the name *God*. And while there are some places in the Bible where *Lord* could be used interchangeably with *God*, that's not the case in the Gospels. See, Jesus didn't go around declaring Himself Lord as in, "I'm divine. I'm God."

The people certainly were not going around calling Him Lord as in *God*. That would've been a crime punishable by death. It would've been blasphemy. When they called Him Lord, when Jesus referred to Himself as Lord, the word used was *kurios*. *Kurios* means "owner of slaves" or "master of slaves." And everyone who heard that word would've thought "master of slaves." Perhaps you think, *All right, Jesus referred to Himself as* kurios, *which means He viewed Himself as a master, but what does that have to do with my relationship with Him?*

There is no such thing as a *kurios* without a *doulos*, or a slave. There is no such thing as calling Jesus Lord without identifying yourself as a slave.

The word *doulos* is used in the New Testament about 130 times. It is most commonly used to describe followers of Jesus. In numerous translations *doulos* appears as "servant," but really the most literal translation is "slave." There are about a half-dozen Greek words that could've been translated as "servant" but *doulos* isn't one of them. The word is slave. And that is certainly how the first-century listeners would've heard this.

So are you living as a *doulos*? Really?

Jesus came to serve, but even more so, Jesus came as a servant. For servants, serving is not just what they do. It is who they are.

So what about you? Is serving something you do? Or someone you are?

REFLECT & DISCUSS

1. Consider the difference between someone who serves occasionally and a servant. Which are

you? There is always value in serving, but you are called to be a servant. In practical terms what does this mean in your life and faith?

2. Self is the biggest hindrance to servanthood. Be honest about the ways self hinders you from fully entering into a life of servanthood. What changes need to be made?

3. What comes to your mind when you think about Jesus as a master? Do you feel oppressed? Energized? Called?

4. Think about Jesus's level of humility. What are some ways you can intentionally choose humility in your life? Live on less? Give more? Serve more?

PRAYER

Lord, when You said, "Follow Me," You invited me into a life of servanthood. Help me to realize that servanthood is the highest calling; it is a life lived in imitation of You. You humbled Yourself in practical and radical ways. Teach me to do the same in my life. You did not consider even equality with God something to be grasped. Show me the things I need to loosen my grip on or let go of completely in order to serve You more fully. Remind me over and over again that greatness in the kingdom of God is not about going higher but about being lower. In Jesus's name.

Part III

A FEW NEW
NOTS TO KEEP
YOU MOVING

Chapter 7

WORSHIPPING TRADITION

As I have considered the Thou Shall life God has called us to live—a life defined by an active faith, not merely by avoiding certain behaviors—ironically I have realized there are a couple of new Thou Shall Nots that do need to be followed. Now, these new Thou Shall Nots are not rules or regulations hidden away in the pages of Scripture that have somehow gone unnoticed by everyone except me. Instead, these Thou Shall Nots are behaviors that inevitably hinder the progress of the life of motion we have been called to live. They each serve as a form of friction.

As I mentioned previously, my first year out of college I served as a preaching intern at a church in Louisville, Kentucky. The salary was meager, but I made the decision to buy a new car. I figured, *I am single, I am poor, why not?* I know, great logic. Only a few months after buying the car I met my future bride, Alex, who lived an hour away from me. Every day for the next six months I drove the sixty miles to and from her house. Obviously the miles added up quickly. About nine months later I started noticing the oil light in my car occasionally flashing on and off but didn't think much of it. The car was new, so I just figured there was a short in the wire or something. Surely the car was not actually warning me the oil was running low. Again, great logic. I will never forget the evening I was interviewing for my first full-time ministry position. Alex had taken the car to visit some friends in the area and planned to pick me up when I was finished. When I called her after the interview I was surprised when she answered the phone in tears. Through the sniffles she explained that she wasn't sure what was wrong but that the car wouldn't move. Then she continued by saying, "It is making a loud noise, and the man at the gas station thinks the engine is blown."

I caught a ride to the gas station and watched in disbelief as the tow truck pulled my *brand-new* car out of the lot and toward the local car dealership. The next morning the mechanic called me and said, "Sir, you need to come down to the lot. I need to show you something." I appreciated his request, but trying to show me something wrong on a car is an exercise in futility. I know nothing about cars except how to fill up the gas and how to get the oil changed. An hour at the nearest Jiffy Lube and $29.95 usually do the trick. Nonetheless I agreed to go down to the lot because the phrase "I need to show you something" is usually not an indication of great news. A little while later the mechanic used a lot of terms I didn't understand as he pointed his flashlight into the engine. All the while I stood nodding as if I actually understood what was being said. I might as well have been having a conversation with a rocket scientist about the latest advancements in astrophysiologistics (yes, I made up that word). After getting a translation, I learned my car had been empty of oil for several months, and indeed the engine was blown.

That week I learned a very hard and expensive lesson: friction is the enemy of motion.

What is true physically is oftentimes also true spiritually. Spiritually speaking, friction is the enemy of motion. Unfortunately there are times in the Christian life when we simply choose to ignore friction, and other times we might pretend it doesn't exist. I think there is a greater issue. I think many of us live our lives unaware. I drove down the interstate day after day, night after night, all the while unaware of the friction that would eventually bring my car to a sudden stop. The same can happen in our faith.

Friction will inhibit us not only from staying in motion but more significantly from staying on mission. The potential sources of friction are many, but I've chosen to focus on four that seem to far outweigh the others.

You are likely going to be surprised at the simplicity of the friction areas I am going to address, but each is more dangerous than it may appear. Consider each one of these areas as a warning light on the dashboard of your faith. Perhaps as you read you will notice one of these lights flashing. If so, please do not assume there is actually nothing wrong. Instead assume that through the knot in your stomach or the lump in your throat, God is trying to tell you something. His intention is not to wag His heavenly finger at you for potential friction that is slowing down your faith but to smooth out the friction by nudging you to make necessary corrections.

Without further ado, the first new Not is "Worshipping Tradition."

CHURCH TRADITION

Church tradition is beautiful, except when it is not.

Before I can really explain what I mean, we need to come to an understanding of the phrase *church tradition*. Simply at the mention of it, a wide array of emotions might be unleashed depending on experience. Some people hear "church tradition" and immediately tense up a bit, ready to go to battle because no one is going to infringe on their church traditions and get away with it without a fight. Others immediately become sentimental as their hearts and minds are filled with thoughts, memories, and images from their childhood growing up in the small country church at the intersection of those two dirt roads. Still others hear the phrase and it makes their skin crawl because they, too, think back to childhood memories from the church, but they aren't warm and fuzzy; their memories of church are filled with guilt and shame and boredom. And some immediately disconnect emotionally when they hear those words because they do not place any value on tradition of any kind.

So what is church tradition? *Tradition* simply means thoughts, behaviors, values, or habits that are passed down from one generation to the next. So, *church tradition* is simply thoughts, behaviors, values, or habits of the church that get passed down from one generation to another—sometimes intentionally, sometimes unintentionally.

Interestingly, within the confines of the church, the concept of tradition is most often associated with music. For decades, the conversation about traditional music versus contemporary music has been lively to say the least. What's really interesting, however, is that the words *traditional* and *contemporary* are both very relative words.

They are moving targets. What seems traditional in one setting would seem extremely contemporary in another setting, and what seems über-contemporary in one setting would seem über-traditional in others.

For the purpose of this discussion about church tradition, I used music as the illustration, but I am talking about something much larger. Church tradition refers to a literally endless list of items, thoughts, behaviors, values, and habits that get passed down from one generation to the next. We can become protective and defensive when tradition gets talked about because the natural assumption is that the specific tradition we value is the one being targeted. To allow us all to be at ease, let me flesh out the phrase just a bit.

Church tradition involves pews and movable chairs and theater seats. It is stained-glass windows and pictures of Jesus and Communion tables. Church tradition is Sunday school and potluck meals and Vacation Bible School; choir robes and baptismal robes; formal attire and casual attire; pulpits and music stands; bulletins and newsletters. The list could go on and on and on.

I meant it when I said at the beginning of this section that there is something beautiful about church tradition—and tradition in general.

My favorite part of the day is when I get to put my little children to bed. Not because I want to get them tucked into their beds and crib and close the door behind me. What I love is the putting-them-to-bed process. For several years before our daughter was born, each night Alex would take one boy and I would take the other, and we would put on their pajamas, read a story, brush their teeth, and then pray with them. When it was my turn to put

Cy to bed, we had a special tradition. We would sing "Jesus Loves Me." When he was a baby I sang that song to him every night. As he grew older we would still rock in the chair, but he would sing the song to me. The song "Jesus Loves Me" is a church tradition; I have never seen the notes written on a page, but the song has been passed from one generation to another, and one day Cy will rock his children to sleep as he sings it to them. You may have never thought about it that way, but that song is a church tradition, and when it is sung by men and women and children of all ages, the only word to describe it is *beautiful*.

I cannot describe the beauty of church tradition, but I know it when I see it.

At its best church tradition, whatever it may be, can enrich our faith, help us connect to God, and remind us of the past while at the same time pointing our eyes to the future.

There are some scenarios, however, when church tradition is far from beautiful. In fact, there are times when it is downright ugly.

THE UGLINESS OF DIVISION

Church tradition is ugly when it *creates division*. And it does. And it does so often. As evidence, if you flipped through the local Yellow Pages and looked under churches, you would literally find hundreds of churches categorized under hundreds of denominations, and in each one of those categories you would find numerous subdenominations. (If you are under thirty, you're probably wondering, *What are Yellow Pages?* It is a really thick book full of yellow pages, and the yellow pages are full of phone numbers ... never mind—just Google "churches" in your community, and you will get the same result.)

I am not in any way condemning the fact that there are many different types of churches; there is room for multiple churches and denominations. The sad reality is that much of the division and subdivision you see in the Christian world is a result of church tradition. There are certainly many denominations that have been created over theological differences, but surely there are just as many that have been created as a result of differing traditions. You observe numerous choices of churches in your community and may think that multiplication has happened, but in reality division has occurred.

You may know all too well about churches that have split over the color of the carpet or the version of the Bible that is used or the design of the building or the time of the services or the style of the music.

Division for any reason should grieve followers of Jesus because it grieves Jesus. In John 17 we are given a front-row seat to listen to a prayer between Jesus and His Father. Jesus prayed this prayer hours before the armed guards came to arrest Him and ultimately hang Him on a cross to die. Since He was facing torture and execution, you might expect Jesus to pray for comfort and protection. But His prayer had nothing to do with His own comfort and protection.

Speaking about the church, Jesus said, "I pray also for those who will believe in me through their message, that all of them may be one, Father, just as you are in me and I am in you. May they also be in us so that the world may believe that you have sent me" (vv. 20–21).

Hours before Jesus was going to die, He prayed that His church would be one. Church unity was not some peripheral issue that was tucked far away in the back of Jesus's mind; it was the issue closest to His heart as He bowed and prayed in the shadow of the cross. Jesus explained why unity matters in that prayer: He said, "May they also be in us *so that the world may believe that you have sent me*." When we as a church are unified despite our differences of opinions on the subject of man-made traditions, the world around us will believe that Jesus is who He says He is.

The other side of that same coin scares me. If being unified means the world will believe in Jesus, then when there is division in the church, the world will doubt that Jesus is who He says He is. Do you see why Satan loves division in the church? He doesn't get his kicks by causing division just for the sake of division; he causes division because it results in fewer people following Jesus. I am sure Satan is thrilled when churches experience disunity because of disagreement about some interpretation of Scripture, but I bet his favorite thing is when we become divided over temporary issues that have absolutely no impact in eternity.

THE UGLINESS OF DISTRACTION

Church tradition is ugly when it *causes distraction* from what really matters most.

Recently I heard a story about a church in Lexington, Kentucky. In this particular church the Communion table sat at the front of the sanctuary. For years the Communion trays were covered with a white sheet on Sunday mornings, and when it was time to serve

Communion, the white sheet was removed. Well, at some point along the way, someone decided to no longer cover the trays with a white sheet. It seems like a harmless decision, but it wasn't. When the decision was made to stop using the white sheet over the Communion trays, arguments erupted, voices were raised, accusations were made, and some people even left the church.

Because of all the controversy, someone decided to research how and when churches starting covering the sacraments with white sheets. This person learned that the practice started in country churches that didn't have air-conditioning. During the hot months these churches would open the windows, which meant flies would occasionally come in, and so to keep the flies away, someone started laying white sheets over the bread and juice. Over time the white sheets that were once simply used to keep flies away became more important than the Communion itself.

That story is true, but even more so it is an accurate metaphor for how tradition oftentimes leads to distraction. Traditions get started with the best of intentions—many times because they meet a practical need—and yet unintentionally the tradition becomes a distraction from what matters most. It may look different in different churches, but when the white sheets get put away, we can get so wrapped up in missing the white sheets that we miss out on Communion.

It is easy to tell these stories when they are about other people, but really these issues are "us" issues. The truth is, whether you can identify with them or not, all of us have certain traditions that we hold in high esteem, and that is okay. But let me offer this word of caution: at some point along this journey, take the time to honestly evaluate the traditions you hold near and dear. After you do your evaluation, make the decision now that the tradition you love, whatever it may be, will never, never, never cause your heart and mind to be distracted from what and who really matters most.

Perhaps it is the Communion table or the stained-glass windows or the drums or hymns or pews. Whatever it may be, enjoy it and allow it to deepen your worship and enrich your faith, but do not allow it to become a distraction.

The way to know if a tradition has become something much more than it should be is by asking yourself this question: What if the tradition I hold dear came to an end? How would I respond? Your answer to that question will expose if you need to evaluate in your heart what really matters.

When any tradition, whatever it may be, is allowed to cause division or create distraction, it is a symptom that the tradition has become something much more than it was ever intended to be. It has gone from being an aspect of worship to being the object of worship.

When time, energy, and attention is consumed with keeping all the traditional ducks in a row, there is simply not enough left to stay on mission.

Sometimes having the right perspective changes everything, and when it comes to church tradition, I think perspective is usually the real issue. With the very best of intentions we create traditions, follow traditions, and continue to pass on traditions. This is all fine, but very subtly we can lose perspective. And that's when traditions change from being an aspect of worship to being the object of worship.

Now, an issue like this one is a bit difficult to address because you might think I am specifically talking about the tradition you love. You may hear me saying we should not value tradition of any kind at all—but that is not my message.

Here is what I am saying: as Christians, may we never allow tradition, whatever it may be, to define us, to rule us, to divide us, or to distract us from what matters most and who matters most. Along any journey of faith, inevitably some traditions will come and some traditions will go; some will end and some will begin. Traditions come and go, but the Truth always stays the same, and the truth is not a what; the Truth is a who. His name is Jesus.

Jesus has sent us on a mission—a mission that calls us to be in perpetual motion. We cannot possibly fulfill the mission of Jesus when we become more focused on tradition than transformation. When policies matter more than people, movement will gradually—or not so gradually—slow to a stop.

REFLECT & DISCUSS

1. What church tradition do you hold near and dear? A song? A worship style? An Easter or Christmas production? A certain version of the Bible? A formal invitation offered at the end of the sermon?

2. After identifying the tradition or traditions you value deeply, spend some time reflecting on whether they are an aspect of your worship or an object of your worship.

3. If the tradition you value the deepest was removed or replaced, how would you respond? Could you still worship? Would you still worship?

4. Ask someone you trust to hold you accountable
so that you will always keep church traditions in
their appropriate place in your faith.

PRAYER

Father, I thank You for the beautiful church traditions that have been handed down from one generation to another. At times traditions deepen my worship of You, and yet I know that all too easily, traditions can transition from being an aspect of my worship to being the object of my worship. Forgive me for the times I have allowed tradition to create division and animosity within Your church body. Traditions are valuable, but You are so much more. Traditions are beautiful, but You are so much more. Remind me to always be more concerned with transformation than tradition. In Jesus's name.

Chapter 8

BEING NEARSIGHTED

If you have ever been to an eye doctor to get your vision checked, you know the routine. You are led back into a dimly lit room where you are asked to sit down in a chair that looks like it belongs in the cockpit of a 747. I find it interesting that while most devices are getting smaller and smaller in this technological age, that eye-test contraption seems to just get bigger and bigger. Once you sit down in the 747 seat, the doctor grabs the mechanical arm of the eye-test contraption and inches it closer and closer to your face until finally your chin settles on the rest. Now, you know what happens at that point—lenses are placed over your eyes one at a time, and then the question comes: "Which is better? Number one or number two? Number two or number three?

I don't know about you, but when the doctor starts asking those questions, my palms get a little sweaty and my pulse starts to race because I feel like I am taking a pop quiz I didn't study for. At first there is usually a vast difference between numbers one and two, but after a few rounds of questioning, I am pretty sure they are just putting the same lens in front of my eye over and over again just to see what I will say. It really bothers me when they ask, "Are you sure?"

"No, I am not sure at all. I don't have a clue which one is better. You're the doctor—why don't you tell me which one is better?"

I am never surprised by the results of the vision test. It is merely a reminder of something I already know: I am nearsighted. After the eye doctor asks me to read the chart on the wall, he usually just moves on to the next portion of the test once I tell him the giant *E* on the top line is a little fuzzy.

When I say I am nearsighted, I mean I am extremely nearsighted. Both of my eyes are a -7.50, so I wear contacts on a daily basis. I do have a pair of glasses, but they are so thick they could easily be mistaken for telescopes. More likely I would be mistaken for Mr. Magoo. There are some obvious disadvantages to being nearsighted, but generally speaking it is not a debilitating condition. People with severe nearsightedness have accomplished incredible feats all throughout human history.

Franklin Delano Roosevelt is considered by many to be one of the greatest presidents in the history of the United States, and yet his sight was severely impaired.

Helen Keller was the first blind and deaf individual to graduate from college.

Claude Monet is considered to be one of the finest painters the world has ever known, and yet during the final season of his life, when he did some of his finest work, his eyesight had diminished nearly to the point of total blindness.

Harriet Tubman helped hundreds of slaves escape to freedom through the Underground Railroad, and yet her vision was severely impaired as a result of a vicious blow to the head.

The list of influential men and women with imperfect vision could go on and on, but the simple truth is that even if you're extremely nearsighted, and even if you're blind, you can do and be almost anything you want—with one exception: if you are spiritually nearsighted, you cannot truly be the church.

From its inception, the church was always intended to have twenty-twenty vision, metaphorically speaking. We were designed to be a community of people loved by Jesus and in love with Jesus who would have the vision to see the needs of other people and the willingness to meet those needs. Maybe the best way to say it is that as the church we were designed to be a people who would have the ability to see beyond ourselves. That has always been the intention for the church, but that has not always been carried out by the church.

In 1917 the Russian Revolution threatened to overtake the city of Petrograd. There was intense fighting and rioting in the streets. Meanwhile, just two blocks away from the actual fighting was the Orthodox church, and leaders from all over the nation were inside, debating heatedly about what color robes they should wear.

In the 1940s many church leaders in Germany refused to take a biblical stand against the Nazi regime. In the most extreme cases the church even endorsed some Nazi policies.

In the 1950s and '60s, during the civil rights movement, the church—in many places, in many ways—turned its head away from the rampant abuse, racism, and discrimination that saturated American culture.

I know those are extreme scenarios, and it would be unfair to paint the whole history of the church with that brushstroke. However, the reality is that these are real chapters in the history of the church, and they are shameful. I have often wondered what Jesus would say when the church fails to be who He called us to be.

In Matthew 5, we see Jesus teaching what we often refer to as the Sermon on the Mount. When Jesus first shared those words, they were sort of like a vision statement of what His church would be like and how His followers would live.

Jesus said, "You are the salt of the earth. But if the salt loses its saltiness, how can it be made salty again? It is no longer good for anything, except to be thrown out and trampled underfoot" (v. 13). *The Message* puts it this way: "You're here to be salt-seasoning that brings out the God-flavors of this earth."

The purpose of salt is quite simple: it is designed to bring out the natural flavors of food. So in a world of desperation, we as the church are to bring out the flavor of hope. In a world of oppression, the flavor of freedom. In a world of anxiety, the flavor of peace. And in a world dominated by hatred, we bring the flavor of love.

The one place that salt is completely ineffective is inside the protective confines of a saltshaker. Just setting the saltshaker on the table does not make anyone's meal taste better. In the same way, as Christians we are no good when we fail to make it outside the safe confines of the four church walls. Not just on a physical level, but on a missional level.

Now, technically speaking, salt does not ever lose its saltiness. But Jesus used this word picture to teach an important principle. The church, just like salt, has a very distinct purpose and mission. Whenever the church loses sight of that mission and becomes something else—like a social club or a theological debate society—it becomes as worthless as salt would be if it lost its saltiness.

If He used the analogy of nearsightedness, Jesus might put it this way: "You are designed to have a heart and an eye for others, but if you lose the ability to see beyond yourself, what good are you?" Spiritual nearsightedness acts as friction, which will quickly slow down a life of faith in motion, eventually bringing it to a screeching halt.

There are a couple of possible ways to respond to times when the church fails to be what Christ intended. We can be tempted to simply wag our finger in disappointment—I have at times struggled against having that response. We can be tempted to rationalize the situation away, somehow trying to explain that there is more to the story. But I think the better way to treat stories from our history as a church—and present-day disappointments—is to view them as cautionary tales. As Socrates taught, "If you don't learn from history, you are bound to repeat it." Though some chapters in the history of the church are absolutely worth repeating, others we should avoid repeating at all costs. How tragic it would be if fifty years from now someone said, "Look at this generation of Christians—for all those years they lost the ability to see beyond themselves. When their neighborhood was unraveling at the seams, they were always huddling together behind the walls of the building. When people were dying of hunger, they were too busy scheduling another potluck dinner to notice. As AIDS was destroying entire countries, their prayer lists were full of people with the common cold."

May you and I never become so nearsighted that we see, talk about, and care about only what happens inside the walls of a church building. May we never lose the ability to see beyond ourselves, because when we stop seeing beyond ourselves, we stop being the church.

I have been wearing corrective lenses of some kind now for almost twenty years. I was in third grade when I went to get my vision checked and the doctor explained that I needed glasses. Until the doctor told me, I wasn't aware that I was nearsighted, because impaired vision was normal for me. I believe the same thing happens in the church at times. Slowly we grow nearsighted and lose the ability to see beyond ourselves, but it just seems normal—so normal that we do not even know we are suffering from the condition. After that initial diagnosis of nearsightedness, I have had my eyes checked once per year, every year. Maybe we in the church would do well to have our vision checked every now and then.

For a few moments, let's pretend we are in a dimly lit room, getting our eyes checked. Not physically but spiritually. Go ahead and rest your chin on the chin rest.

I am going to give two options in each pair. You will have no problem reading the words, but as you read them, decide honestly which of the statements describes your thoughts, emotions, passions, concerns, and priorities the best:

> #1 When your needs are unmet, you are inclined
>   to speak up.
> #2 When someone else's needs are unmet, you view
>   it as an opportunity to serve.

> #3 People of all shapes, sizes, and colors matter to
>   you because they matter to God.

#4 People who do not look like you, act like you, or speak like you matter less to you than those who do.

#5 You lose sleep at night because your favorite sports team lost.

#6 You lose sleep at night thinking of those who do not have a place to sleep at night.

#7 Poverty is an issue you take personally because you care about the welfare of people.

#8 Poverty is an issue for the government welfare system to handle.

#9 You struggle at times with being nearsighted.

#10 You think only other people struggle with being nearsighted.

You can pull your chin off the chin rest now. So, how did you do? My guess is that most of us are at least slightly nearsighted. There is value in confessing that. I'll be the first to say it: at times I can be spiritually nearsighted. Sometimes my needs matter more to me than the needs of others. Sometimes I think my opinions and thoughts are the most valuable.

If you are nearsighted and readily admit it, God can correct your vision. We are always going to be a work in progress; we are always going to be learning to see the world from God's perspective, learning to see beyond ourselves.

But I get concerned when people think spiritual nearsightedness is just a struggle other people deal with. When you think this, your condition has gotten very serious. When you get to the point where you wouldn't even recognize the big *E* on top of the chart, you may be almost blind.

If spiritual nearsightedness is causing friction in your life and has inevitably slowed your faith, you do not have to settle for going completely spiritually blind. The same Jesus who once healed blind eyes physically still heals blind eyes spiritually. The question is not whether Jesus can heal your spiritual nearsightedness—but whether you will allow Him to.

I hope you will.

REFLECT & DISCUSS

1. As you read, did you conclude that you struggle with a level of spiritual nearsightedness?
2. Fifty years from now, what might people say in regard to what you missed, ignored, or were too nearsighted to notice?
3. If you have become aware of spiritual nearsightedness, make intentional commitments about how you are going to begin seeing beyond yourself.

PRAYER

Father, forgive me for the times I fail to see beyond myself. I know I am called to be salt and light, which requires me to have my eyes set on others. Allow me to develop spiritual twenty-twenty vision so I will recognize the opportunities to serve, love, and care that exist in my community and beyond. Do not let me be content to wait fifty years to look back and see what and whom I missed; instead give me eyes to see now. Thank You for giving me such a lofty task—to act as a change agent in this world on Your behalf. When I fail to see beyond myself, may I always turn back and repent, then open my eyes again. I know You are the healer of sight, not just physically but spiritually. Heal me, Lord. In Jesus's name.

Chapter 9

PRETENDING

An iPhone application called "Confession" acts as a digital confession booth. Users can choose the category of sin they have committed or the command they have broken, then confess and receive penance. If the sin they committed isn't already on the list, the application allows people to add options so there is an opportunity to confess any and every kind of sin. This app reminds users when their last confession was and which sins they have previously confessed.

I would not personally endorse the "Confessions" app, but it is healthy to regularly confess our sin to God. Confessing sin serves as a gentle, humbling reminder that we are not perfect.

For a long time, the church has been called out for being imperfect. In the face of accusations, our human tendency is to become offended. We rationalize our behavior, turn the focus away from ourselves, and attack other groups, organizations, or faith movements to point out their imperfections. But the appropriate response is to just come clean. Like it or not, we as Christians have been rightfully accused.

My wife and I have two young boys—Cy is six, and Cruz is four. They have wild and creative imaginations, so we spend a lot of time pretending. We have a variety of costumes and hats and other apparel in our house, but the best ones are the Buzz Lightyear and Woody costumes from *Toy Story*. When my boys are wearing those costumes, don't you dare call them by their real names—you will be not so nicely corrected about their "true" identities. It gets really complicated when, while wearing one character's costume, they pretend to be another character. So Cy might be wearing the Woody costume, but when I say, "Hi, Woody," he will tell me, "I am not Woody—I am Peter Pan!" All of the pretending gets a little confusing, but we just go along with it because it's cute, innocent fun that is good for the imagination.

As humans grow older, we never really lose our fascination with pretending. We may grow out of the Buzz and Woody or super-hero costumes, but it seems like we never grow out of pretending. Whether in school, at work, or in relationships, most of us have numerous masks we wear depending upon the circumstances.

We want others to think we are successful or popular, so we wear that mask.

We want others to believe we are a really great parent, so we have that mask.

We want to convince others we are happy and content, so we keep that mask handy.

We want others to believe we are super spiritual, so we have that mask.

Pretending is really cute and fun for children, but when it comes to grown adults, it is ugly and dangerous.

For generations, most people had a basic sense of reverence or respect for the church, but for a lot of reasons that is not really the case anymore. Today, if you asked people you encountered to say the first word that comes to mind when they hear the word *church*, you might not like what you would hear. A lot of people hear *church* and think *boring* or *irrelevant* or *intolerant*. But if you could dialogue further with the same people about their disdain for the church, at some point in that conversation you would probably hear the word *hypocrisy*. To that accusation I would say yes and no. When most people accuse the church of hypocrisy, they do so with an inaccurate understanding of what hypocrisy really is. They are trying to communicate that the church is full of sinners, which is true. Here is where the misunderstanding happens. Struggling with sin, which we all do and always will in this life, does not make us hypocrites. But at the same time, hypocrisy according to the accurate definition is a real issue in the church. A hypocrite is not someone who struggles with sin; a hypocrite is someone who pretends he or she doesn't struggle with sin.

The word *hypocrite* is actually derived from Greek theater. One actor would play several different characters during a production, and to switch roles he would simply put on a new mask every time he went onto the stage. Therefore, a hypocrite is someone who is always hiding behind a mask, always pretending to be something or someone he is not. Maybe the best definition for *hypocrite* is simply … pretender.

According to that definition, hypocrisy is a real issue in the church, but it is nothing new; pretending has always been a struggle for religious people.

If you study Jesus's life and ministry, you will quickly find there was one category of people He didn't get along with. It was not tax collectors, though they were considered to be scum; it was not prostitutes; it was not the down-and-outers of society. It was the religious elite. If you are new to Christianity or reading the Bible, it probably sounds strange that Jesus didn't get along with the religious elite. After all, Jesus was a rabbi, He was the Son of God, He inspired the writing of the Bible, and so you would naturally assume that He would be fond of the religious elite. Instead, the religious elite were often on the receiving end of words from Jesus that weren't exactly warm and fuzzy. In Matthew 23 we are given a front-row seat as Jesus shares His feelings about a group of religious leaders called the Pharisees. In that day if you were a Pharisee you were on the Who's Who list of society; you were on the top rung of the leaders. As a Pharisee you were well educated, wealthy, and well respected by almost everyone ... except for Jesus. Simply put, here was Jesus's issue with many of the religious elite: they were fakes, they were phonies, they were pretenders.

So in Matthew 23, as Jesus was speaking to crowds of people and also to His inner circle of disciples, He began unleashing His feelings about the teachers of the law and the Pharisees. Within just a few short paragraphs, Jesus accused the Pharisees of being hypocrites seven times. For the Pharisees there was no greater imaginable insult than being called a hypocrite. Remember I said that the word *hypocrite* was the word used for an actor in a Greek play? Well, the Pharisees claimed to be too righteous to ever attend Greek theater—it was beneath them—and so when Jesus referred to them as hypocrites, it was a punch in the gut. While Jesus didn't call these religious leaders hypocrites to get under their skin or to insult them, I think it was the most accurate word He could use to describe their lives.

In Matthew 23:5–7 Jesus said this about the Pharisees:

> Everything they do is done for people to see: They make their phylacteries wide and the tassels on their garments long; they love the place of honor at banquets and the most important seats in the synagogues; they love to be greeted with respect in the marketplaces and to be called "Rabbi" by others.

Phylacteries were small boxes that the Pharisees tied to their wrists and around their foreheads, and inside these boxes they kept small pieces of Scripture. In Deuteronomy 11:18, God instructed the Israelites this way: "Fix these words of mine in your hearts and minds; tie them as symbols on your hands and bind them on your foreheads."

God had instructed His people to keep Scripture on their hands and on their heads, and the Pharisees were doing just that, so where is the issue? Well, read between the lines of Jesus's words to understand the problem: He said, "They make their phylacteries wide." In other words, they made their boxes extra large so that everyone knew they were super religious. The Old Testament also taught the people to wear tassels on their cloaks as a reminder of God's commandments, but Jesus pointed out, "The tassels on their garments [are] long." The purpose of wearing Scripture on their heads and hands and tassels on their garments was to keep them faithful, and yet they had turned it into a show. That is what playactors do, right?

Later in the passage Jesus said,

> Woe to you, teachers of the law and Pharisees, you
> hypocrites! You are like whitewashed tombs, which
> look beautiful on the outside but on the inside
> are full of the bones of the dead and everything
> unclean. In the same way, on the outside you appear
> to people as righteous but on the inside you are full
> of hypocrisy and wickedness. (vv. 27–28)

In the Jewish world it was not kosher for a person to go near a
dead body, because it would make them unclean. Many historical
scholars say that during certain festivals and celebrations, such as
Passover, the tombs in Jerusalem were covered with white paint so
that people would not accidentally run into one and become unclean.
Jesus was basically telling the Pharisees, "You wear nice costumes,
you put on a nice religious act, but on the inside, behind the mask,
it is a different story."

Throughout chapter 23 Jesus accused the Pharisees over and over
again of being hypocrites and gave them specific examples of how.
But the theme of His message was this: you are fake, you are actors,
you are pretenders.

As you read Jesus's words about the Pharisees, it is easy to shake
your head in disappointment at the religious leaders. You may find
yourself wondering, *Shouldn't they have known better than anyone else
that God is not impressed by religious playacting?* After all, they were
experts in Old Testament law; many of them would have had the
entire Old Testament memorized word for word. You would think

they would have known better than anyone that God is about honesty and transparency, but they didn't. So as you read Matthew 23, your natural inclination will be to shake your head and point your finger in disgust and disappointment at the religious leaders—but if that is your only response, you will have missed out on the teaching moment.

It is time to come clean. The religious leaders in the first century are not the only ones who have ever settled for spiritual pretending. Trust me, I know. I spent the first part of my life on the stage of religion, pretending to be something that I was not. I knew the rules, I could quote more Scripture than most other people my age, I never missed church, I always dressed the right way when I went. On the outside I was very religious. I didn't wear phylacteries or tassels, but I am telling you if I would have, they would have been wide and long. People would have noticed. I would have made sure they did. And it would be really easy to talk about my religious pretending as if it were something I struggled with only in the past, but I still struggle sometimes.

I am not proud of it, but there are times when I say what I think people want to hear me say. There are times when I act certain ways because I am a pastor and people expect it of me. I admit there are times I have said or done or agreed to things because I knew it would make me look holier than I really am.

There are times when I am guilty of hiding behind a mask, when I have settled for pretending.

Perhaps you find my confession disappointing because you have certain expectations of a pastor and author and I fall short of those expectations. Or maybe this is the first time you have experienced a pastor admitting imperfection in such a vulnerable way, and so you may find my confession refreshing. But more likely the reason you find my confession refreshing is because you just learned you are not the only one who occasionally hides behind a mask.

Let's consider three symptoms of being a spiritual pretender.

PRAISE OF PEOPLE

You are a spiritual pretender *if praise from people matters more to you than the pleasure of God*. Some people spend their whole lives in the church, and everything they do and say is a performance. Like Jesus said to the religious leaders in Matthew 23:5, "Everything they do is done for people to see." Perhaps you teach a class or hand out bulletins or volunteer in the nursery. All are admirable, and all are necessary, but if you do those things for the applause of people instead of doing so to please God, you are just performing on a stage. You are a pretender.

EXTERNAL APPEARANCE

You are a spiritual pretender *if external appearance matters more to you than internal character*. In our culture, we are trained to measure people's value based almost solely upon what they look like. That is why most of the people who end up on the front of popular magazines all have the right dimensions and figures. Every year *People* magazine does the "50 Most Beautiful People" issue. I have never seen them do a "50 Most Honest People" issue. If we are not careful, we can measure people by appearance within the confines of the church, too. Very easily we can start measuring the spiritual depth of a person by style of hair, body piercings, tattoos, and, perhaps more than anything else, dress style.

Some people feel that if their hair is the right length and they are dressed to the nines, this somehow translates into having the right heart for God. Others haven't washed their hair in two weeks and are dressed in jeans, T-shirts, and sandals and feel that *this* reveals their authenticity for God. It is a two-way street; there can be equal arrogance on both sides. There is great danger when we begin to feel superior to others because of something as shallow as what we wear or when we look down on others because of what they choose to put on.

If someone wants to wear a suit and tie and you are quietly judging him because you feel that by dressing down, you are somehow being more "real" for God, then shame on you. You are a pretender.

If you see someone dressed down and you secretly find yourself casting judgment that they must not be all that serious about God, then shame on you. You are a pretender. God is not more impressed with a tie than a T-shirt; dress pants are not more spiritual than jeans. If it's your opinion that they are, remember you didn't get that idea from Scripture.

RULE FOLLOWER

You are a spiritual pretender *if you are more consumed with following the rules than following Jesus*. In the first century, no one knew the law better than the Pharisees, and no one followed the law better than the Pharisees. As I told you earlier, most of them had the entire Old

Testament memorized word for word, and most of them lived out the law to the dot of the *i* and the cross of the *t*. The problem is that many of them were so wrapped up in the letter of the law that they totally ignored the spirit of the law. Jesus put it this way: "You give a tenth of your spices—mint, dill and cumin. But you have neglected the more important matters of the law—justice, mercy and faithfulness. You should have practiced the latter, without neglecting the former" (Matt. 23:23). The circumstances may be different now, but the scenario is the same. It is possible to get so wrapped up in following rules that you totally ignore the call to follow Jesus.

- You can memorize all the passages in the Bible about the least and the lost but never invest your life in them.
- You can give 10 percent of your income in the offering every week and still give God 0 percent of your heart and soul and mind.
- You can go to church every week and still not be the church during the week.

If you are infatuated with following the rules but not as interested in following Jesus, whatever that may look like, you are a pretender.

Pretenders will be sure to pray before their meals in public if they know someone is watching. Pretenders are quick to chastise the entertainment choices of their friends, family, and coworkers but would be red in the face if people knew about the shows on their DVR. Pretenders feed the hungry and help the needy as long as there is an audience to notice; when there isn't, they don't. Pretenders assume everyone is concerned with their preferences and desires, though they have no interest in the preferences and desires of others. Pretenders may celebrate the success of others on the outside but on the inside are disappointed and jealous. Pretenders work harder at trying to convince others they have a solid marriage and family than actually working to nurture a solid marriage and family. Pretenders think they are spiritually superior because of the long list of rules they keep tucked away in their back pocket and are always sure to follow. Pretenders think right now I must be describing someone else.

I am a recovering pretender; I have spent time living behind the mask. Have you? Are you? Maybe your act has impressed some people along the way, but Jesus is not impressed. It is time to take off the costumes; it is time to put down the masks.

When you live behind a mask, it is impossible to live a life that really honors God. You will be far too consumed with keeping up your external religious image to have any time or energy to focus on the vast needs and opportunities that abound all around you. When you are living behind a mask, you will avoid certain people you think might tarnish your image or get your shirt wrinkled or your shoes scuffed. When you are hiding behind a mask, you are going to be too concerned about impressing the large crowds to focus on the needs of just one who usually goes unnoticed.

REFLECT & DISCUSS

1. All of us have a tendency to wear masks occasionally. What masks are you tempted to

wear? Who do you try to impress with your pretending? Family? Friends? Coworkers? Your church community?

2. Being real is rare but beautiful. Choose two people who know you the best and love you the most and ask them to hold you accountable in terms of pretending. Ask them to be lovingly honest when they notice you pretending to be something or someone other than who you really are.

3. After you have identified a mask you often wear, ask yourself why. Do you feel pressure? Do you wonder what people will think if they really knew? Do you worry you will lose relationships that matter to you? Know this: the One who knows who you really are and what you are really like—the One who knows you the best—also loves you the most and will never leave you or forsake you. So take off the mask.

PRAYER

Father, even as an adult I am consumed with pretending. Give me the strength and courage to put the mask down and be honest about who I am. But also give me the grace to grow beyond where I currently am. The growing I need to do will never take place if I am hiding behind a mask, so when I am tempted to pretend, nudge me, convict me, stop me. Thank You for loving me just the way I am, but also for loving me too much to leave me this way. I cannot possibly live in motion and on mission when I am consumed with pretending to be someone or something else. So for the sake of the mission, Lord, I commit to put down the masks and get real. In Jesus's name.

Chapter 10

JUDGING THE WRONG PEOPLE

I don't know about you, but when I am driving down the road or stopped at a red light, I am often amused by the bumper stickers people put on their cars. You can find out almost anything you want to know about people from their bumper stickers. I say bumper stickers plural because they seem kind of like Lay's chips and tattoos ... apparently you can't have just one. People say that doing everything in moderation is the secret to life, but when it comes to bumper stickers that principle usually goes out the window. A hundred bumper stickers seems a bit unnecessary, but I must confess I do kind of like it—it provides me with free entertainment.

I have not done any scientific research to prove this, but it seems like one of the most popular bumper stickers is the one that says, "My child is an honor student." And now I am seeing more and more bumper stickers that say, "My child can beat up your honor student." So much pent-up aggression these days.

In the sea of bumper stickers, there are a few I find to be quite amusing:

- "Isn't a smoking area in a restaurant like a pee-ing area in a swimming pool?" (When you think about it, quite profound.)
- "The more people I meet, the more I like my dog." (I don't get it, either.)
- "I love cats … they taste just like chicken." (I do not know this from experience.)

There are a lot of bumper stickers that amuse me, but there are others I don't find so amusing. Maybe you have seen the bumper sticker that says, "Jesus, please protect me from Your followers." From a public-relations aspect, the church has seen better days. As we discussed in the previous chapter, one of the reasons people would give for not liking the church is the apparent hypocrisy, and we acknowledged that at times we struggle with pretending to be something we are not. But while many people's biggest issue with the church is the apparent hypocrisy, other people would say, "The church is too judgmental." I understand why some people feel like that, because unfortunately in some ways it's true. As a church we have the reputation of carrying around a Bible in one hand and a gavel in the other. It is all too easy for us as Christians to become the self-appointed judge and jury, serving as the voice of judgment in everyone else's life.

JUDGE AND JURY

When I was in junior high and high school, I wore the same outfit to school every single day. Now, I know a junior high boy wearing the same clothes every day is not exactly shocking—I mean, it seems that once boys turn fourteen, they become anti–personal hygiene overnight—so I should explain what I mean. I didn't literally wear the same outfit every day, but figuratively speaking, every day I wore a black robe. I was a little Judge Judy in disguise. As a kid who had grown up in an ultra conservative, legalistic church, I viewed it as my personal responsibility to play the role of judge in everyone else's life. I didn't stand on street corners with signs that said, "God hates people," but I was always willing and ready to speak—oftentimes harshly—about the sin I recognized in other people's lives. And so as conversations took place around me about the latest drunken party or the newly released profanity-laced R-rated movie that everyone was planning to see, I was always listening and lurking, just waiting for an opportunity to throw my two cents' worth of judgment into the conversation.

Now, I should say that in playing the role of judge, I really did have the very best of intentions. I felt like it was my role as a Christian to expose the sin in everyone else's life. Unfortunately, the way I lived, with my finger always pointing and the gavel always pounding, reaffirmed what a lot of people already believed about the church: the church is too judgmental.

However, when it comes to judging, I am not sure if being *too* judgmental is really our biggest problem. Though there are instances when as a church we are too judgmental—and I don't think any of

us would deny that—I think our bigger issue is that at times we are
not judgmental enough.

Do I have your attention now?

THE WRONG KIND OF JUDGING

Generally speaking, judging is one of the most misunderstood
concepts in the Bible. Most people both inside and outside the
church are inclined to believe that as Christians, we should never
judge anyone for any reason. After all, Jesus is the One who said in
Matthew 7:1, "Do not judge, or you too will be judged." That is one
of the verses quoted most by people who are not in the church, but
I wonder if those same people know anything about the rest of the
passage? When you read that verse in context, along with many other
New Testament passages, you find that judging is not prohibited, but
it is restricted.

Before we dive into this, we first need to agree on a definition
for *judging*. As I have considered the text and the context of the
biblical passages, I think the best way to summarize judging is this
way: "honestly and lovingly addressing sin in another person's life."

The New Testament teaches that as Christians we do have the
responsibility to judge according to that definition; the problem
is that we tend to judge all the wrong people. Maybe you are an
exception to the rule—and I hope you are—but many Christians
do most of their judging outside of the church. When I say *church*
I am not talking in terms of a place but a people. Many Christians
tend to gravitate toward judging the lives of people who do not even
claim to be followers of Jesus. In most cases I think people do it with

the very best of intentions. Just like I did when I was a teenager, these Christians subconsciously feel like it is their responsibility to point out sin when they see it—as if their "sin radar" has gone off, prompting them to speak. Now, do not misunderstand me: there is absolutely a time and place as a Christian to share the truth of God's Word with people outside the church, but our first and foremost responsibility is not to do sin management. Though we can certainly stand up and even speak out about truth, it is important that we do not reduce ourselves to being moral police officers.

When we are dealing with someone who is living outside of a relationship with Jesus, our goal should not be to help him or her become a nicer person or a more morally upright person. Our goal is to lead that person into a relationship with Jesus. When we lose sight of that end goal, instead focusing on keeping the moral score for people outside the church or simply making sure they follow all the right rules, we are just making sure that hell is full of really well-behaved people. But when we focus on loving people into a relationship with Jesus, we are making sure that heaven is filled to capacity.

THE RIGHT KIND OF JUDGING

What business is it of mine to judge those outside the church? Are you not to judge those inside? God will judge those outside.

(1 Cor. 5:12–13)

We can learn a lot from the early Christians. They lived in a culture and under a government system riddled with sin. Marriage was held in low esteem; sexual excess was openly approved and applauded; homosexuality was endorsed and celebrated. Infanticide was an acceptable form of family planning. The Colosseum was regularly filled with bloodthirsty cheering as brutal persecution and murder took place before all the people watching. As for Christians, there were no charitable deductions, property tax exemptions, freedom of speech protections—just the constant threat of persecution.

Yet the New Testament is strangely silent when it comes to harsh judgments and condemnations of the Roman government, its leaders, or its soldiers. While it does speak of societal decadence in general, it usually does so in the context of reminding Christians to no longer live that way.

The reason was simple. The early church understood that their job was not to judge and condemn the pagans around them. They knew their job was to win them over with love.

Generally speaking, we as the church tend to be quick to blow the whistle when our non-Christian neighbor or coworker or family member is wrapped in sin, but too many times when a follower of Jesus is involved in blatant sin, instead of having an honest conversation, we just stay quiet and put the whistle in our pocket.

It is not our responsibility as Christians to judge the sin of those living outside the church, but we absolutely have the responsibility to speak honestly about sin in the lives of fellow Christians.

The apostle Paul wrote two letters to the first-century church in the city of Corinth. We know from his first letter that the church was becoming saturated by blatant, intentional sin. Apparently the Corinthian Christians were sort of turning their heads from the sin. I don't know if they were just hoping that it would go away on its own or simply trying to avoid a difficult conversation, but whatever the reason, they were not openly addressing the sin problem. Read what Paul wrote to the church:

> I wrote you in my earlier letter that you shouldn't make yourselves at home among the sexually promiscuous. I didn't mean that you should have nothing at all to do with outsiders of that sort. Or with crooks, whether blue- or white-collar. Or with spiritual phonies, for that matter. You'd have to leave the world entirely to do that! But I *am* saying that you shouldn't act as if everything is just fine when a friend who claims to be a Christian is promiscuous or crooked, is flip with God or rude to friends, gets drunk or becomes greedy and predatory. You can't just go along with this, treating it as acceptable behavior. I'm not responsible for what the *outsiders* do, but don't we have some responsibility for those within our community of believers? God decides on the outsiders, but we need to decide when our brothers and sisters are out of line and, if necessary, clean house. (1 Cor. 5:9–13 MSG)

In this letter Paul not so subtly reprimands these Christians for being so tolerant of sin in the church. These people were showing up for worship services every Sunday, they were gathering for small-group meetings, they were sharing potluck dinners together—and they knew there was blatant sin in their midst. Yet instead of having an honest, difficult conversation with the appropriate people about the sin, they were just tolerating it. Instead of judging the obvious sin, they were just winking at it.

I wish I could say this example of sin tolerance was just an isolated incident in the church, but unfortunately it is a pretty familiar scenario.

- A Christian woman decides to divorce her Christian husband because he just isn't meeting her needs anymore, and instead of reminding her of what God says about divorce and nudging her in the direction of reconciliation, her Christian friends hug her and say, "We understand; sometimes marriages just don't work out." They may not realize it, but by refusing to speak the difficult truth, the Christian friends are winking at sin.

- A young Christian couple is living together, and though they intend to get married, they are not married yet. The other people in their community group know that their choices are not honoring God, but instead of warning the young couple about the seriousness of sexual sin, they just ignore it because they know the couple really cannot afford to live separately. The motivation of the community group members may be good, but by choosing to ignore the situation, they are winking at sin.

And the scenario plays out all the time with gossip and pride and self-righteousness. We see the sin, we know about the sin … and more often than we may like to admit, we just turn and look the other way.

When we recognize sin in the life of a fellow Christian, all too often the temptation is just to wait and hope that someone else will pick up the gavel. We hope that someone else will have the difficult conversation so we don't have to. But if everyone is always waiting on everyone else to have the conversation, the conversation never happens, and the sin continues to flourish and grow.

As Christians we have the responsibility to speak honestly about sin.

Now, let me offer you this precaution: if you are going to have honest, difficult conversations about sin in the life of a fellow Christian, there are some stipulations.

EXAMINE YOUR OWN LIFE

First, before you speak you need to *examine your own life for sin.* I think this is the issue that keeps a lot of Christians from having the difficult conversation about sin with someone else. They think, *Well, who am I to talk to someone else about sin? I am just a sinner saved by grace too.* That is true, but we need to make an important distinction: yes, we all wrestle with sin—there is no escaping that reality. But there is a difference between occasionally falling into sin and intentionally, knowingly choosing sin as a lifestyle. In Matthew 7:3–5 Jesus said,

> Why do you look at the speck of sawdust in your
> brother's eye and pay no attention to the plank in

your own eye? How can you say to your brother, "Let me take the speck out of your eye," when all the time there is a plank in your own eye? You hypocrite, first take the plank out of your own eye, and then you will see clearly to remove the speck from your brother's eye.

Jesus teaches that if you are involved in an extramarital affair, please do not bother speaking to the man in your Sunday school class about his habit of getting drunk. If you are secretly embezzling money from your company, do not speak to someone else about their struggle with pornography. If you knowingly cheat on your taxes, do not speak to the woman in your Bible study about her gossip problem.

The principle is simple: if you knowingly have a log in your own eye, do not try to take the speck out of your brother's or sister's eye.

Examine your own life for intentional sin before you speak to your fellow Christian, but once you have done so, be willing to have a difficult, probably uncomfortable conversation.

THE RIGHT MOTIVATION

Second, you need to *address sin with the right motivation in mind*. The reason judging has such a negative connotation—especially in regard to the church—is because most people associate judging with condemnation. And unfortunately, that has often been the motivation behind exposing or addressing sin. One too many times we have initiated a conversation about sin with the wrong tone and for the wrong purpose. Paul explained the appropriate motivation for addressing sin in the lives of fellow Christians:

> You must not simply look the other way and hope it goes away on its own. Bring it out in the open and deal with it in the authority of Jesus our Master. Assemble the community—I'll be present in spirit with you and our Master Jesus will be present in power. Hold this man's conduct up to public scrutiny. Let him defend it if he can! But if he can't, then out with him! It will be totally devastating to him, of course, and embarrassing to you. But better devastation and embarrassment than damnation. You want him on his feet and forgiven before the Master on the Day of Judgment. (1 Cor. 5:3–5 MSG)

And so as Christians, the motivation for speaking honestly about sin should never be condemnation but restoration. And though restoration is the appropriate motivation for speaking about sin, at the center of the conversation is an even deeper motivation: love for people.

I say that because I think one of the reasons we often hesitate to have the difficult conversation about sin is because we really love the other person and do not want to risk ruining the relationship. Listen, loving someone deeply is not a reason to avoid the hard conversations; it is the reason to have the hard conversations.

If I saw my six-year-old son, Cy, riding his bike in the street and noticed a car speeding toward him, I wouldn't hint at the fact that he needed to get out of the street, and I wouldn't hope that someone else would tell him in time. No, instead I would run to him as fast as I could and tackle him out of the way. Tackling him out in the street might hurt him, but it also just might save him. That is the way we should envision conversations about sin. When someone you really love is in danger, you don't just turn and look the other way, hoping it all turns out all right; you do whatever it takes to get him or her out of danger. Sometimes the best thing you can do is pick up a phone or walk to the next office or invite a friend over for dinner and initiate an honest, loving conversation about sin. The conversation may hurt the one you love, but it just might save them too. Not only will dealing honestly with sin potentially save someone from harm but it will also help ensure that the person stays on mission and in motion. Nothing brings the healthy movement of faith to a screeching halt quicker than sin.

In college I had a weekend preaching ministry at a small country church. There were only about a hundred citizens in the town, including cows and stray dogs, and there were about fifty people in the church. As you can imagine everyone knew everyone, and everyone knew everyone's business. Well, one weekend I found out that a deacon in the church, who was a single man, had been allowing a woman to live in his house with him—and when I say live in his house with him, I don't mean just live in his house with him.

I tried to come up with any reasonable idea about how I could get out of talking to him about it, but I knew it was unavoidable. I will never forget that conversation. My heart was pounding, my palms were sweating, and my voice was probably even shaking because he was this big, burly, hairy man ... and I'm not ... and I didn't know how it was going to play out. I remember telling him he needed to make a lifestyle change of some kind. I explained that he either needed to marry the woman or force her to move out of his home. At that point I expected him to get a bit angry or defensive, but instead he began nodding his head in agreement, and tears rolled down his cheeks. He acknowledged that the situation wasn't right and that he knew it had to change. We discussed how he was going to handle it, we prayed together, and then much to my surprise the conversation ended with a hug (of course, it was kind of a half hug because that is what men do). It was one of the most difficult conversations I have ever had, and yet one of the most rewarding. Within a few weeks of that conversation, the man and woman repented of their sin, they married each other, and they continued to be faithful members of the church. As a Christian and a minister, I have had conversations like that one a few other times. They are rarely easy, but I have never regretted one of them.

Here is what I do regret: the times I should have started a conversation about sin but didn't. I have to confess that part of the reason those conversations that never happened haunt me is because I cannot help but wonder: What if, when I was walking a dangerous path littered with sin and needed someone to have a difficult conversation with me more than I needed my next breath, everyone just walked by and winked at me instead?

I am not in any way suggesting you spend your life wagging a finger and banging the gavel; I am suggesting you spend your life loving people when and where they really need it the most—when they are walking a dangerous path littered with sin. Sometimes the most loving thing you could do is to have an honest conversation about sin.

Our God didn't ignore our sin, and He didn't just look the other way. Maybe you have never thought about it this way, but we follow a God who started a difficult conversation about our sin—and it began this way: "Father, forgive them, for they know not what they do." Jesus spoke those words as He hung on a cross, dying for our sin. God didn't just wink at our sin; He offered to wipe it away.

THE FRICTION

Let me connect the dots between judging and our discussion of sources of friction in our faith. Judging the right people the right way is a responsibility of being a Christian. Being willing to speak honestly about sin in others and allowing others to speak honestly about sin in our own lives allows us to more effectively stay on mission and in motion. However, judging the wrong people the wrong way will eventually bring the healthy motion of the Christian life to a halt. How can you possibly spend any time or resources reaching out to, caring for, and investing in people when both hands are busy keeping score on the tally sheet of sin?

REFLECT & DISCUSS

1. Many Christians are quick to judge the wrong people the wrong way but hesitant to judge the right people the right way. Why?

2. What excuses have you found yourself struggling with that have hindered you from honest, loving conversations about sin?

3. Reflect on why it is impossible to live in motion and on mission while carrying a gavel around.

4. Be intentional about surrounding yourself with people who are willing to speak honestly with you about sin.

PRAYER

Father, let me seriously take the responsibility of holding fellow believers accountable for sin. May I always do so with the spirit of restoration and healing. Forgive me for the times when I have seen sin in someone's life and yet refused to say anything. When I am willing to address sin, I help ensure that people stay on mission. So, Father, give me the strength, courage, and love to deal honestly with sin. With those who are not yet following You, remind me not to become consumed with their sin but to become consumed with sharing You so they can be saved from their sin. In Jesus's name.

Part IV

NOT JUST THE
END, BUT THE
BEGINNING

Chapter 11

CONSIDER THE SOURCE

Go. Act. Advocate. Serve.

Considered alone, these words can seem demanding, harsh, and burdensome. But you have to consider the source: God. Considering the source here requires us to go a bit deeper, because there are so many misperceptions about God. These words will feel distinctly different depending on how you primarily view God.

Sometimes our view of God is contrary to who the Bible says He is.

There are so many words and images in the Bible that describe the characteristics of God and shape our understanding of what a relationship with Him looks like. The Bible uses words like *Creator, King, Master,* and *Shepherd* to form a collage of who God is and what He is like. To leave any of those ideas out would mean falling short of capturing who He is.

In the New Testament, there is one word used more than any other—over 150 times—to describe God: *Father*. It is almost like He was a broken record when the New Testament was being written. In almost every book, on almost every page, you see God being called "Father." God is Creator, He is King, He is Master, He is Lord, He is the Great Physician, He is the Judge, He is the Alpha and Omega, the Beginning and the End—He is all of those and more—but if He wears a name tag, I am convinced that it would say, "Hello I Am Father."

If I asked you to speak the first words that come to your mind when I said "Father," some of you would speak words of respect and admiration, but many of you would not. Maybe instead, you hear "Father" and immediately associate that title with words like *absent, angry, abusive, distant, intimidating, preoccupied*. I know some of you have been outstanding fathers who have loved, cherished, appreciated, taken care of, and protected your families, and I am so thankful for men like you—I am trying to be a man like you—but there are so many fathers in our society who haven't stepped up to the task. And so we take our experience or understanding of *Father*, whether good or bad, and we project it on God. If your father was distant, you just naturally assume that God is too. If your father was angry, you assume God has a short fuse too. If your father was preoccupied, you assume God is preoccupied. If your father had better things to do than invest in you, you assume God has better things to do as well. If your father was disappointed in you, you assume God is disappointed in you.

If you believe that God is too busy for you, is angry with you, is distant from you, is disappointed in you, or wants nothing to do with you, please hear this: you have been lied to, and Satan was the author of that lie. My guess is that if you have believed any of those lies, your life is probably coming apart at the seams. Satan uses lies like those to steal, kill, and destroy. Maybe you have become convinced that prayer is pointless because God is not listening anyway. Perhaps you have concluded that studying the Bible is futile because God used to offer healing but doesn't anymore. And maybe some of you are tempted to wander away from the church because you are wondering if God's grace could ever cover what you have done. You have been lied to, so let me set the record straight: God is preoccupied … with you. If He had a desk, your picture would be on it. If He had a wallet, your picture would be in it. God is not disappointed in you; He is captivated by you—the Bible says you are the apple of His eye. God is not distant; He is literally closer than your next breath.

God is Father. God is not an angry, distant, or busy Father … He is a loving Father. That is His identity, and His identity has everything to with our identity as followers of Jesus. If God is a loving Father, then you and I are loved children. I know that sounds so simple, but I also know that if we really know and understand and believe that we are loved by God, everything about who we are changes. God's love transforms insecurities into certainties. God's love changes fear to hope. God's love washes stained hearts as white as snow. God's love renews joy and reignites passion for living. God's love is patient and kind. God's love never fails; in fact the Bible says His love endures forever. God's love keeps promises, protects innocence, and provides strength. God loves in a way that only He can, because love isn't just something He does; it is who He is. For us, love is a virtue to be sought after or gained, but for God, it is His identity.

One Christian author put it like this:

> If we continue to picture God as a small-minded
> bookkeeper, a customs officer rifling through our
> moral suitcase, as a policeman with a club who is
> going to bat us over the head every time we stumble
> and fall, or as a whimsical, capricious, and cantan-
> kerous thief who delights in raining on our parade
> and stealing our joy, we flatly deny what John wrote
> in his first letter … God is Love.[1]

In the Bible God went out of His way to make sure we would understand the nature of the relationship He desires to share with us: it is not just Creator/created, not just Master/servant, not only Teacher/student—first and foremost it is a Father/child relationship. That is why when Jesus taught His disciples to pray, the very first two words He spoke were, "Our Father." For His disciples, that was earth-shattering language. They would have never dared to speak about God or to God with such casual yet intimate language. The English word *Father* used in that verse is actually the Aramaic word *Abba*. A more accurate translation of *Abba* is "Daddy."

Most babies say a few simple words by the end of the first twelve months of life. And one of the first words normally spoken at that age is *da-da, da*, and then finally *daddy*.[2] A little Jewish child that age in first-century Palestine would begin to say *ab-ab, ab, Abba*. When Jesus tells us to address God as "Abba," or "Daddy," He crushes the walls of religiosity that often keep us feeling so distant from God; with one word He redefines what it means to be in a relationship with God. By calling Himself Daddy, God doesn't just ask us to bow at His feet; He invites us to curl up on His lap. When you understand that God thinks about you and loves you like a father loves a baby on his lap, everything changes.

Including how you receive the words *Go, Act, Advocate,* and *Serve.*

Coming from a "do-whatever-I-say-or-else" Father, these commands would seem demanding, harsh, and burdensome.

Coming from an "I-am-keeping-score-on-you" Father, these commands would seem intimidating, demoralizing, and unfair.

However, coming from an "I-love-you-so-much-I-have-gone-to-a-red-bloodstained-cross-and-back-so-I-can-share-My-life-and-My-mission-with-you" Father, these words become a matter of opportunity, privilege, and joy.

REFLECT & DISCUSS

1. If you were to describe the way you view God, what words would you choose? Angry Tyrant? Scorekeeper? Cosmic Policeman? Loving Father?

2. However you have viewed God up to this point, pray specifically about developing a more accurate understanding of who He is. Ask God to reveal Himself to you as your loving Father.

3. How has your view of God affected your expression of faith? What changes need to occur in light of who He really is and what He is really like?

PRAYER

Father, may I learn what it means to have You as Father. You are my loving Father, and so I am a loved child. That perspective of You changes everything, including how I receive Your commands to Go, Act, Advocate, and Serve. Give me the vision to see You for who You really are and then to respond accordingly. Thank You for the privilege You have given me to carry out Your will on earth as it is in heaven. In Jesus's name.

Chapter 12

ONE MORE WORD

In a conversation with Jesus, words like Go, Act, Advocate, and Serve would come rolling off of His tongue, but not first, and not last. In regard to His relationship with us, I think there is one more word He would want us to hear Him whispering before and after all others.

In John 15 we find Jesus sharing a few final moments with His disciples before He goes to the cross. It was a Thursday evening, and He had just shared what is often referred to as the Last Supper with His disciples. After doing so Jesus led His disciples on a journey toward the garden of Gethsemane, where He spent time agonizing in prayer about His impending suffering and death. On the way, He stopped and spoke these words to them—and to us:

> I am the true vine, and My Father is the vinedresser. Every branch in Me that does not bear fruit, He takes away; and every branch that bears fruit, He prunes it so that it may bear more fruit. You are already clean because of the word which I have

spoken to you. Abide in Me, and I in you. As the branch cannot bear fruit of itself unless it abides in the vine, so neither can you unless you abide in Me. I am the vine, you are the branches; he who abides in Me and I in him, he bears much fruit, for apart from Me you can do nothing. If anyone does not abide in Me, he is thrown away as a branch and dries up; and they gather them, and cast them into the fire and they are burned. If you abide in Me, and My words abide in you, ask whatever you wish, and it will be done for you. My Father is glorified by this, that you bear much fruit, and so prove to be My disciples. (John 15:1–8 NASB)

Am I the only one who noticed that Jesus sounds like a broken record in that passage?

Abide.

Abide.

Abide.

If you read the entire John 15 narrative, you find the word *abide* used ten times in eleven verses. As I began this book I posed this question: "What are God's favorite words?" But perhaps the better question is, "What is God's favorite word?" Can I take the liberty to make a suggestion?

Abide.

Remember, when Jesus spoke these words He was only hours from the cross. Continuously sprinkled throughout some of His last words before His death is this one word: *abide.*

Abide is a verb, but honestly it is a bit of a boring verb. Though *abide* technically is a verb, it is not one that calls for drastic, radical action of any kind. It is a word more about being than doing. But the struggle for many people, including me, is that we tend to think more in terms of doing than being. And so even if you want to abide, you just need this one question answered first: Jesus, what should I do?

Abide.

Yeah, I know, I get that, Jesus—but what I should I do?

Abide.

The imagery Jesus used is so crucial to understanding what it is to abide. He said, "I am the vine, you are the branches." So to understand what Jesus is asking of us—actually commanding us— we have to take a close look at the relationship between a vine and its branches.

The vine is the source of strength, power, and nutrients—it is the source of life. A branch can grow fruit only when connected to the vine. Or, to put it a different way, a branch can fulfill its mission and purpose only when connected to the vine. There is no fruit outside of a connection to the vine. There is no life outside of a connection to the vine. A branch has one simple role in the relationship: to remain connected to the vine. To abide. The branch does not need to wear itself out with any effort to grow, grow, grow. The branch simply must abide. Any activity, such as growth, would only be a result of connection to the vine.

To abide is simply a matter of remaining, which means there is a strange irony to the mission and purpose God has in mind for our lives. We are to stay, we are to be still—so we can grow and flourish and move.

The irony is exposed in this question: Are we to be still or to be in motion?

The answer? Yes.

If you are a follower of Jesus, then you are a branch. So am I. Because we are branches, any fruitful activity is only and always a result of staying connected to the Vine. If we become disconnected from the Vine, any activity intended to honor God will be nothing more and nothing less than a flurry of religious activity. The relationship provides the meaning and motivation for the activity.

Fulfilling the mission and purpose God has for our lives begins and ends in relationship with Him. He is the source of power, courage, strength, wisdom, vitality, fruit, and life. However, being in relationship with God is not a means to an end—relationship with God is the end.

And so if we were to ask God to fill in the blank "Thou Shall _____," I think there are many words and phrases He would use. But first and last I am convinced He would say, "Thou Shall Abide." It is not a threat but the greatest invitation one could ever be given.

And so as you abide,

Go,

Act,

Advocate,

and Serve.

REFLECT & DISCUSS

1. *Abide* sounds so easy and yet at times feels so difficult. As you evaluate your life, what are

the obstacles that keep you from abiding with Christ as He desires? Busyness? Sin? Worry?

2. Identify some lifestyle changes you could make that would allow you to slow down and more intentionally abide with Christ regularly.

3. Only as you abide will you effectively be able to Go, Act, Advocate, and Serve. Therefore, place your highest focus on abiding with Christ, and these other commands will be the natural fruit of that connection.

PRAYER

Father, You invite me to abide. Help me understand that my role in relationship with You is simply to stay connected to the Vine. I am so prone to rely on my own strength and ability, which is why I am so quick to grow weary. There is a great task at hand, which can only be accomplished as I abide. Draw me near. Keep me near. When I drift, lovingly draw me back to Your side. You are the Vine, I am the branch—may I always and only abide in You and with You. As I do, I will Go, Act, Advocate, and Serve. All in Jesus's name.

NOTES

CHAPTER 1: FAVORITE WORDS

1. Exodus 20:3–17 ASV.

CHAPTER 3: GO

1. George Barna, *How to Turn Around Your Church* (Ventura, CA: The Barna Group), DVD.

2. Philip Yancey, *The Jesus I Never Knew* (Grand Rapids, MI: Zondervan, 2002), 230.

CHAPTER 11: CONSIDER THE SOURCE

1. Brennan Manning, *The Furious Longing of God* (Colorado Springs: David C Cook, 2009), 77.

2. *Your Baby's First Words*, WebMD, www.webmd.com/parenting/guide/baby -talk-your-babys-first-words.